College Questions ... in Arithmetic, Grammar, Geography, History, Spelling, and Drawing

COLLEGE QUESTIONS

PART I.

The Examination Papers of 1888, 1889, 1890, 1891,
1892, 1893.

PART II.

The Examination Papers of 1894, 1895, 1896, 1897,
1898, 1899

IN

ARITHMETIC, GRAMMAR, GEOGRAPHY, HISTORY, SPELLING, AND DRAWING

AN AID IN PREPARING FOR

ENTRANCE EXAMINATIONS TO HIGH SCHOOLS, NORMAL COLLEGE,
COLLEGE OF THE CITY OF NEW YORK, WEST POINT, ANNAPOLIS,
THE CIVIL SERVICE AND THE REGENTS' EXAMINATIONS

Harry Newman

FOURTH EDITION

NEW YORK
WILLIAM BEVERLEY HARISON
5 WEST EIGHTEENTH STREET

Copyright, 1899.

By WILLIAM BEVERLEY HARISON.

ARITHMETIC.

1. (a) When is a common fraction said to be in its lowest terms ?

(b) When are four numbers said to form a proportion ?

(c) What is meant by the present worth of a sum of money due six months hence ?

(d) What is a minuend ? a subtrahend ? a quotient ?

2. (a) Reduce to its simplest form the following expression :

$$\frac{\frac{3}{4} \text{ of } 2\frac{1}{4} \text{ of } \frac{3}{8}}{\frac{2}{7} \text{ of } 3\frac{1}{2}} \times \frac{\frac{3}{8}}{\frac{2}{3}} + 4\frac{1}{3}$$

(b) Add together (using the least Common Dividend) $\frac{3}{4}, \frac{4}{5}, \frac{1}{2}, \frac{5}{8}.$

(c) Divide $1\frac{3}{4}$ by $\dfrac{\frac{3}{8}}{\frac{3}{16}}$

3. (a) What is the effect of multiplying the denominator of a fraction by a whole number ?

(b) Explain the reason of this.

4. (a) Write in decimal form :

Forty hundred thousandths.

Nine hundred and twenty-four millionths.

Two thousand, one hundred and twelve thousandths.

(b) Divide 5.6 by .00014.

(c) Reduce $\frac{3}{120}$ to a decimal.

5. (a) Add the following decimals : 3.123, .00084, 200.1.

(b) Subtract 2.0046 from 3.3.

(c) Multiply 1.001 by 33.0004.

(d) What denominator is always understood with every decimal fraction ?

3

6. (*a*) What is the effect upon the value of a decimal fraction of moving the decimal point one place to the right ?

(*b*) Explain the reason of this.

7. If it costs $100 to carpet a room 24 feet long and 21 feet wide with carpet of a certain quality, how much will it cost to carpet a room which is 31 feet 6 inches long, and 18 feet wide, with carpet worth 20% more per yard ?

8. A dealer bought in the country 500 bushels of potatoes for 50 cents a bushel and shipped them to New York for sale. The freight was 2½ cents per bushel; cartage in New York on the whole was. $7.50, and one-tenth of them were damaged on the way so as to be unsalable. At what price per bushel must he sell the remainder so as neither to make nor lose on the transaction ?

9. A man spends 25% of his capital for a house, puts 60% of the remainder into his business, and invests the rest in bonds bearing 6% interest. From these bonds he receives an income of $1,200 per annum. What is his entire capital ?

10. A, B, and C can together do a piece of work in 3 days. A alone can do it in 12 days : and B. alone can do it in 6 days. In how many days can C alone do it ?

ENGLISH.

1. Use each of the following words in a separate sentence, showing the correct use of the word :

(*a*) Betrayed ; (*b*) apparent; (*c*) faltering ; (*d*) sympathy ; (*e*) anonymous.

2. (*a*) What is a participle ? Give an example of an imperfect participle.

(*b*) What is the comparative degree of adjectives ? Give the comparative of "*ill*."

(*c*) What are modes or moods ? What mood is employed in the example "*if he were*"?

(*d*) How do intransitive and passive verbs differ ? Write a sentence of at least ten words, using an intransitive verb as the predicate.

(e) State the difference between an interrogative and a relative pronoun. Construct a sentence showing the use of both pronouns.

3. Construct a compound sentence of not less than twenty words, one of the clauses of which shall be complex.

4. Construct a complex sentence of not less than fifteen words; with an infinitive phrase as the subject.

5. Analyze the following :

"Trust no Future, howe'er pleasant !
Let the dead Past bury its dead ! "

6. Analyze the following :

"In the middle of the night, and under all the rest of our distresses, one of the men, that had been down on purpose to see, cried out we had sprung a leak."

7. The following examples, showing the careless use of language in advertisements, are from an article in *Chambers' Journal*. You are required to correct the errors and give a short reason for the corrections.

(a) A shop in Cheapside warns everybody against unscrupulous persons "who infringe our title to deceive the public."

(b) The proprietor of an eating-house near the docks has on his door the notice to the gallant tars who frequent the port : "Sailors' vitals cooked here."

(c) A boarding-house keeper announces in one of the papers that "he has a cottage to let containing eight rooms and an acre of land."

(d) A dealer in cheap shoes makes this announcement. "Ladies wishing these cheap shoes will do well to call soon as they will not last long."

(e) The same carelessness appears in the following : "This hotel will be kept open by a widow of the former landlady who died last summer on a new and improved plan."

8. Write a short letter, the body of which shall not be less than twelve lines in length, properly dated, addressed

to your uncle, and signed Thomas Gilbert; announcing that your father is about to sail for Europe; mentioning the length of time he is likely to be absent and the countries he intends to visit, and adding such other particulars as would be proper in a letter of this sort.

GEOGRAPHY.

1. (*a*) Sketch an outline map of the United States, omitting Alaska.

(*b*) Locate on this map the following ranges of mountains: Blue, Cumberland, Coast Range, Sierra Nevada, Cascade.

(*c*) Locate on the same map the following rivers and lakes: Missouri, Mississippi, Hudson, Lake Michigan, Lake Erie.

(*d*) Locate on the same map the following cities: Boston, Chicago, New Orleans, San Francisco, Galveston, Philadelphia, Buffalo, St. Louis, Washington, Charleston.

2. From what State or States do we obtain silver, copper, gold, mercury, petroleum, salt, sugar, cotton, rice, wheat?

3. Through what waters and near what countries would you pass in the most direct course, (*a*) from New York to Odessa? (*b*) from San Francisco to Calcutta?

4. (*a*) What is the highest portion of the continent of Asia?

(*b*) What is the most northerly portion of the mainland of Europe?

(*c*) Which is the larger, the Caspian Sea or Lake Superior?

(*d*) Does the Volga feed or drain the Caspian Sea?

(*e*) What mountain ranges or elevations of land determine the general directions of the rivers of North America?

5. (*a*) What is the size and form of the earth?

(*b*) What is physical geography?

(*c*) What is meant by longitude?

(*d*) What is the latitude of New York City?

(*e*) Explain the phenomena of day and night.

HISTORY.

1. Give an account of the voyages of Columbus. Why was not the New World named after him ?

2. State when, where, and why the "Pilgrim Fathers" settled in America.

3. Name the several wars, with dates, in which the colonists took part, down to the Revolution. Which was most important and why ?

4. Give the names of the thirteen colonies and group them according to their governments ; charter, proprietary, etc. Were the people of the colonies alike in nationality, religion, or other respects ? State the differences.

5. Describe the events of the Revolutionary War in the South in the year 1780. Full account.

6. What were the causes of the Mexican War ? What part did General Scott take in it ?

7. Valley Forge, Wyoming, Lookout Mountain, Appomattox, Tippecanoe, Carteret, Wayne, Seward, Burr, Meade. Why are these names of places and persons prominent in our history ?

8. Name the Presidents of the United States, and give dates, from Madison to Buchanan, inclusive. Give the principal events of Jackson's administration.

9. Give the Southern and Northern views of the secession question.

10. What is the Federal Constitution ? Give a full history of its adoption ; why, where, and when.

SPELLING.

Capacity is an *absolute necessity* of *naval command*, as the fate of the Spanish Armada *signally* showed, and the most *patrician communities* have one by one been *compelled* to *yield* up the *claims* of rank and *descent* in the command of the sea. It is the *arena* where new men can rise to power, and among the Vikings were men who felt this and rose *accordingly*. Hence the *difficulty* of *identifying* the *greatest* among them in that ninth *century,* when they were in the midst of the *destructive* work that *preceded settlement* and *occupancy.*

An attack of ague.	An arbitrary decision.
The skilful artisan.	A prolific brain.
Anxious thoughts.	Triumphant shouts.
Individual peculiarities.	Wholesome correction.
A disastrous engagement.	A handsome legacy.
Lincoln.	Idaho.
Bismarck.	Amherst.
Teneriffe.	Boulogne.
Sumatra.	Hebrides.

Normal College.

ARITHMETIC.

1. Define quantity, number, figure. Explain the difference between number and figure. Explain briefly the Roman method of notation. Write the present year in Roman characters. What is a common fraction? Upon what does the value of a fraction depend? Why are fractions reduced to a common denominator before they can be added?

2. A man has $20\frac{2}{4}$ acres in one field, $40\frac{4}{5}$ acres in another, and $\frac{2}{3}$ as many acres in a third as in the other two; how many has he altogether?

3. What is ratio? What is proportion? Why must the first and second terms of a proportion be of the same name or kind?

It requires $\frac{1}{8}$ of a bushel of oats to keep 4 horses $\frac{1}{3}$ of a day; how many horses will 9 bushels feed $\frac{2}{5}$ of a day?

4. What is per cent? Write decimally $\frac{1}{8}$ of 1%.

Bought apples at $\frac{1}{3}$ of a cent each and sold them at $\frac{1}{2}$ of a cent each; required the gain per cent.

5. What is the face of a note at 90 days, the proceeds of which, discounted at a bank at 6%, are $2,000?

6. A man bought a house, agreeing to pay $\frac{1}{2}$ in 4 months, $\frac{1}{3}$ in 9 months, and the remainder in a year. Find the average time of credit.

7. Sold $460 uncurrent money at $\frac{1}{2}\%$ discount. Find the discount and market value.

8. What principal will in 3 years, 8 months, 15 days, at 6%, give $76.09½ interest?

ENGLISH.

1. Name the different kinds of pronouns. Write a sentence to illustrate each kind.

Write a sentence with the word *what* used as an adjective.

Correct "Men and Boys Clothing."

2. What is a compound sentence? Write an example? Write a complex sentence. Show the difference between a compound and a complex sentence. Write a compound sentence with four co-ordinate clauses.

3. Write a sentence containing the word *order* as a noun and as a verb. Give an illustration of a descriptive adjective used as a noun; of a numeral adjective used as a noun.

Construct a sentence with a verb in the active voice and change it into the passive voice without altering the meaning.

4. "At the first stage of his journey, a trial of his tenderest feelings awaited him in a public dinner given him at Alexandria, by his neighbors and personal friends, among whom he had lived in the constant interchange of kind offices, and who were so well aware of the practical beneficence of his private character."—*Washington Irving*.

Analyze the above sentence very briefly. Tell the kind of sentence. Write out and number each clause and give the modifiers of *had lived*.

5. Parse *given, him* (after given), *had lived, aware*, and *so*.

GEOGRAPHY.

1. New York is 71° west longitude and San Francisco about 122° west longitude. If it is 9 o'clock A.M. in the former, what o'clock is it in the latter ?

2. Give as near as you can the direction of the following cities from New York : *Mobile, Augusta, Montreal, Naples, Copenhagen, Melbourne, Montevideo, Calcutta, Teheran,* and *Odessa.*

3. Give the capitals of Greece, Switzerland, Egypt, Chili, Peru, Canada, Wisconsin, Georgia, Texas, Vermont.

4. Bound Pennsylvania. Name its capital city ; its largest city and five other cities of importance.

5. Name the States on each side of the Mississippi ; those that border the great lakes ; and those on the Pacific coast.

6. What is latitude ? What is the greatest longitude a place can have ?

7. How can you tell with certainty the "true south ?"

8. What are the general productions of the temperate zone ? of the torrid zone ?

9. Why have great cities as a rule been built on the sea-coast or on rivers ? and what great invention of modern times will perform the duty formerly done by the great rivers ?

10. Why are elevated places cooler than those on the plain ?

11. Name four of the great railroad centres of the United States.

12. Bound France. Name its capital and five of its important cities.

13. On what rivers are the following cities : Delhi, Berlin, Rome, Bagdad, Vienna ?

14. Where would you find Santa Fé, St. Augustine, St. Paul, Sacramento and San José ?

15. Name five mountain ranges in Europe.

16. Name three capes on the coast of North Carolina.

17. Bound the State of Missouri. Name its capital and its largest city.

18. Name six of the great rivers of the United States; state where they rise and into what bodies of water they discharge themselves.

19. Through what waters would a vessel pass in going from Albany, N. Y., to Hartford, Ct. ? Name five cities she would pass by.

20. A city is 10° 30' due north of another city. How many geographical miles are they apart ?

HISTORY.

1. (a) What great idea prompted the discovery of America ?

(b) Give a brief account of the discovery of America by Columbus and of his subsequent voyages.

(c) Write a brief account of the voyages and discoveries of Cartier.

(d) What great Englishman attempted to found settlements in North America in 1583, '84, and '85 ? Name two of the navigators who sailed under his patronage.

(e) What part of North America was claimed by England, and why ?

2. (a) Which one of the original thirteen States was first settled ? When, where, and by whom was it settled ? What was the character of the first settlers ?

(b) What State was settled in 1614 ? By what people was it settled ? How long did they hold possession of it ?

(c) When and by whom was Massachusetts settled ? Describe briefly the character of those people.

(d) Name two of the early Indian wars and state their causes.

(e) What was the cause of King William's war, and by what treaty was it terminated ?

3. (a) What excuse did the English government make in 1764 for taxing the American colonies ? What reason did the colonists assign for resisting taxation ?

(b) Where and when did the Second Colonial Congress meet ? Who was its president ?

(c) Give the important events of 1776 as nearly as you can in chronological order.

(d) Give a brief sketch of Washington, stating when and where born, his education, first employment, military training, and at least three battles of the Revolution in which he figured in person.

(e) Name four distinguished statesmen of the Revolution.

4. (a) What great measure was passed by Congress in 1787 ? What influence had this measure on the growth of the country ?

(b) What is the Federal Constitution ? Who was the first President under this Constitution ?

(c) What territories have the United States purchased at different times, and from whom ?

(d) What "right" did Great Britain claim, which was the chief cause of the war of 1812-15 ?

(e) Name the Presidents in order from Washington to Cleveland, and name those who were re-elected.

5. (a) Who was President during the Mexican War ? Why were a portion of the New England people sternly opposed to this war ? Name three American generals who distinguished themselves in this war.

(b) What celebrated measures were passed by Congress in 1819-20 and 1850 ? How did the admission of Texas and the acquisition of new territory to the Pacific interfere with the celebrated act of 1819-20 ?

(c) What do you mean by a civil war ? From your general reading, name some civil wars that took place in other countries. Why did the South take up arms against the Union ? Why was the North bound to succeed in the long run ? Who was commander-in-chief of all the land and naval forces of the United States from 1861 to 1865 ?

(d) What great fortification was captured by Grant in July, 1863 ? Who was the Confederate commander ? Give a brief account of the capture of this stronghold.

(e) What two great generals were opposed to each other in the series of skirmishes and battles that immediately preceded the capture of Atlanta? Who superseded the Confederate commander at a critical moment? What American hero captured the city of Mobile?

SPELLING.

The *adoption* of the *Federal Constitution* was another *epoch* in the life of Washington. Before the *official* forms of an *election* could be carried into *operation* a *unanimous* sentiment *throughout* the Union *pronounced* him the nation's *choice* for the *presidential* chair. He looked forward to the *possibility* of his election with *characteristic modesty* and *unfeigned reluctance,* as his letters to his *confidential* friends bear *witness.* "It has no *fascinating allurements* for me," writes he to Lafayette. "Let those follow the pursuits of *ambition* who have a *keener relish* for them." In reply to a letter from Colonel Henry Lee, he wrote: "The event to which you *allude* may never happen. This *consideration* alone would *supersede* the *expediency* of announcing any *definitive* and *irrevocable* resolution."

At the *frontier* of *Pennsylvania* he was met by his former *companion* in arms, Mifflin, now Governor of the State, who with Judge Peters and a *civil* and *military escort* was waiting to *receive* him. Washington had hoped to be spared all military *parade,* but found it was not to be *evaded.* At Chester there were *preparations* for a public *entrance* into Philadelphia.

The ladies of Trenton had caused a *triumphal* arch to be erected. It was *entwined* with *evergreens* and *laurels* and bore the *inscription,* "The *defender* of the mothers will be the *protector* of the *daughters.*" Never was *ovation* more *graceful, touching,* and *sincere.* His progress through New Jersey *afforded* a *contrast* to his weary *marchings* to and fro, *harassed* with doubts and *perplexities,* in the time of the Revolution.

College of the City of New York 1889.

ARITHMETIC.

1. (*a*) Define a common fraction :
   (*b*) A compound fraction ;
   (*c*) A decimal fraction ;
   (*d*) Give the rule for the multiplication of one decimal fraction by another. .
   (*e*) What is discount ?

2. (*a*) Add the following fractions : $\frac{3}{4}$ of $\frac{5}{6}$ of $\frac{3}{10}$, $\frac{\frac{4}{7}}{10}$, $\frac{5}{8}$.

   (*b*) Find the value of the following : $\dfrac{2\frac{1}{4}}{3} - \frac{1}{2}$ of $\frac{5}{8} - \dfrac{1\frac{1}{2} \times \frac{7}{8}}{\frac{3}{4} \text{ of } 1\frac{6}{5}}$

3. (*a*) Write in a decimal form : $\frac{3}{10000}$. $\frac{4}{100}$. $\frac{51\frac{5}{8}}{100}$.
   (*b*) How do you most easily multiply a decimal by 10 ?
   (*c*) Divide 16. by 4.; by 400.; by .004.
   (*d*) Multiply 41 by .0006.

4. In multiplying $\frac{3}{4}$ by $\frac{5}{6}$ explain why cancelling the 3 in the numerator and denominator will give a correct result.

5. Divide 3.25 by .5 and explain the reason of the rule for pointing off the decimal places in the quotient.

6. What sum of money put at interest for 2 years 9 months and 9 days, at 6% per annum, will produce $2,951.80 ?

7. A certain cistern can be filled by one pipe in 10 hours, by another in 6 hours, and can be emptied by a third in 5 hours. In how many hours can it be filled if all three pipes are opened at once ?

8. An importer bought in France 1,000 pieces of a certain goods at $40 per piece. The duty paid on importing the goods was 50% of the cost, and the freight and other charges were in all $1,500. For how much per piece must he sell the goods so as to make 20% ?

9. Two men start from two towns 105 miles apart and walk toward each other. They meet at the end of 15 hours.

The first has travelled 3 miles per hour. At what rate has the second travelled ?

10. If 10 men working 8 hours per day can build a certain wall in 6 days, how many hours a day must 12 men work to build the same wall in 4 days ?

ENGLISH.

Analyze the following sentences, 1 and 2. If the candidate prefers to diagram one or both of them he may do so.

1. " In the Acadian land, on the shores of the basin of Minas

Distant, secluded, still, the little village of Grand Pré
Lay in the fruitful valley."

2. " Alas ! the meanest herb that scents the gale,
The lowliest flower that blossoms in the vale
Even where it dies, at Spring's sweet call renews
To second life its odors and its hues."

3. (*a*) What is a sentence ? Name the different kinds of sentences.

(*b*) What is a phrase ? Name the different kinds of phrases.

(*c*) What is the difference between a phrase and a clause ?

(*d*) What is the difference between a compound and a complex sentence ?

4. Correct the errors in the following examples, *a*, *b*, *c*, and *d*, being particular to give in each case the reason for the correction ; and answer the inquiry in *e*.

(*a*) " Who is there ? It is me."

(*b*) " If you had been working all morning like we have you would be glad to rest."

(*c*) " You can't deny but what you received notice."

(*d*) " If any pupil has seen the lost book, I shall be glad if they will let me know."

(*e*) " If he were here, he would answer for himself."

Why is *were* used after *he* ?

5. (*a*) In what ways is the plural of nouns formed ? Give an example of each.

(*b*) Give the feminine of the following nouns : Bachelor, Boy, Drake, Earl, Gander, Ram, Hart, Wizard.

(*c*) What is meant by a part of speech ? What is in- flection in grammar ?

(*d*) What part of speech undergoes the most change by inflection ? Give the singular and plural of one example.

(*e*) What are the two simple rules for the use of the auxiliaries *shall* and *will ?*

GEOGRAPHY.

1. How high is the highest mountain on the earth ? What is the diameter of the earth in miles ?

2. Through what two points on the earth's surface do all meridians pass ? Borneo and Iceland each extending over ten degrees of longitude, which is the longer in miles ?

3. Which State borders on four of the five great lakes ? Which two other States border each on two lakes ?

4. Where are the following European cities (give country, part of country, river or sea in and on which each lies) : Antwerp, Belfast, Copenhagen, Malaga, Palermo, Rouen, Warsaw, Zurich ?

5. Name the European countries of which Algeria, the Azores, Ceylon, Egypt, Greenland, Java, and Victoria, are severally dependencies ?

6. How would you go, eastward, from Vera Cruz to the Philippine Islands ? Through what waters and by what islands would you pass ?

7. Where are the following South American cities : Bahia, Bogota, Callao, Cayenne, Maracaybo, Quito, Rio Janeiro, Valparaiso ?

8. Where are these capes : Hatteras, Land's End, Race, St. Roque ?

9. Where are Anam, Bokhara, the Congo Free State, Corea, Manitoba, Morocco, the Orange Free State, Servia ?

10. Draw a map showing the course of the Mississippi from its source to its mouth. Indicate its junction with its principal tributaries ; mark off the States on both banks and name them, and locate the capitals of these States.

HISTORY.

1. Explain the origin of the names (*a*) "America," (*b*) "United States," (*c*) "New York," (*d*) "Geórgia." State fully why they were applied and when.

2. Describe the colonists of Massachusetts, Pennsylvania, and Maryland, showing in what respects they differed from each other. Include a brief account of their first settlements.

3. Give a sketch of Queen Anne's War. Name the principal Indian wars since 1776, giving dates.

4. Show that the period from 1765 to 1775 was an important one in our history. Give the chief events in order.

5. How far did France assist us in the Revolutionary War ? Who was Steuben ? What services did General Greene render in the struggle ?

6. Washington as President : state all you know respecting his administration, naming events, public measures, cabinet ministers, etc.

7. Who were Marquette, Stuyvesant, Irving, Morse, Warren, Andros, Webster, Seward, Fulton ? Name six of our prominent naval heroes since 1775.

8. Give the substance of the amendments to the Constitution adopted since the Civil War. What other questions were settled by that war ?

9. Give an account of the chief military operations of the year 1863. What bearing did they have on the result ?

10. What is meant by the "Federal Union," and what tie holds it together ? What form of government do we have in this State, and when was it adopted ?

2

SPELLING.

The queen is upon terms of the greatest *cordiality* with Lord Melbourne, and very *naturally*. Everything is new and *delightful* to her. She is *surrounded* with the most *exciting* and *interesting enjoyments ;* her *occupations,* her *pleasures,* her *business,* her *court,* all present an *unceasing* round of *gratifications.* With all her *prudence* and *discretion* she has great animal spirits, and enters into the *magnificent novelties* of her *position* with the *zest* and *curiosity* of a child.

Bachelor.	Electrotype.	Amuse.
Deceit.	Foreign.	Answer.
Decrease.	Centennial.	Dakota.
Appetite.	Doubtful.	Moscow.
Elephant.	Barometer.	Nicaragua.
Acre.	Calico.	Dardanelles.
Bullion.	Furious.	Paraguay.
Recitation.	Agreeable.	Jefferson.
Delicacy.	Cemetery.	Massachusetts.
Behavior.	Advice.	Pennsylvania.

Normal College.

ARITHMETIC.

1. Express as a decimal $\frac{2}{3} \times \dfrac{\frac{3}{4} - (\frac{1}{8} \times \frac{10}{6})}{3\frac{1}{3} - 2\frac{2}{6}}$.

2. A can do a piece of work in $\frac{4}{5}$ of an hour ; B can do $\frac{2}{5}$ of it in one hour. In what time can both do it ?

3. What is the difference between the interest and the time discount of $576 due 16 months hence at 6% ?

4. What decimal of 7 bu. 1 pk. 5 qt. is 82 bu. 3 pk. 1 qt. ?

5. How much can be realized yearly from an investment of $6,900 in a 4½% stock, bought at 86, brokerage ¼% ?

6. The interest on a note for 2 y. 6 mo. at 7% was $118.23. What was the face of the note ?

7. Bought the following bills on 4 months : September 9th, 1880, $140 ; October 9th, $160 ; November 6th, $200. What is the average time of payment ?

8. A merchant sold goods for $150 and lost 10%, whereas he should have gained 30%. How much were they sold under their proper value?

9. If 25 men working 8 hours a day do ⅜ of a piece of work in 24 days, in how many days of 10 hours each will 30 men finish the piece of work?

10. In what time will $12,000 yield $2,500 at 4½%?

ENGLISH.

I.

I am the besom that must sweep the court clean of such filth as thou art. Thou *hast* most traitorously *corrupted* the *youth* of the realm in erecting a grammar school. It will be proved to thy face that thou hast men about thee that usually talk of a noun and a verb, and such abominable words as no Christian ear can endure to hear.   *Henry VI.*

1. What kind of a sentence is the first sentence?

2. What kind of a sentence is the second sentence?

3. What kind of a sentence is the third sentence?

4. In the first sentence write the kind of clauses according to the divisions known as noun, adjective, and adverbial.

5. In the third sentence write the kind of clauses according to the divisions known as noun, adjective, and adverbial.

6. Define *clause* and *phrase*.

7. Parse the following words: *Besom, that* (1), *must, sweep, clean, grammar-school, in, that* (2), *that* (3), *such.*

8. Write the potential mood, past perfect [pluperfect] tense of the verb to *write*.

9. What is a passive verb? How is it formed? Write a compound sentence of three clauses containing the passive voice of the verbs *love, esteem, reverence.*

10. Construct a complex sentence with one adjective and two adverbial clauses.

II.

1. Write a letter of application for a position as teacher in the ward in which you live.

[Credit will be given for *arrangement*, for *correctness* of language, for *punctuation*, for the right use of *capitals*, and for *orthography*.]

2. Define *garrison; instigate, repentance, remorse, hallow*, and use each word in a separate sentence.

3. Punctuate and capitalize the following:

   Trav my lord sir john umfrevile turned me back
   With joyful Tidings and Being Better Horsed
   out rode me after him came spurring hard
   a Gentleman almost forspent with speed
   That stopped by me to breathe his Bloodied Horse
   he asked the way to chester and of him
   I did demand what news from shrewsbury
   he told me that Rebellion had ill luck
   And that Young Harry Percy's spur was cold.

4. Convert the following into simple sentences:

   " When I had done this I returned."

   " I came that I might assist you."

   Correct the following and give reason:

   " The reveries of a batchelor " were written by D. G. Mitchell.

GEOGRAPHY.

1. How many degrees from the Equator to the Tropic of Cancer ? What is the width of the North Temperate Zone ? What is the latitude of New York ? Name three important cities in Europe having nearly the same latitude.

2. From what countries does the United States import coffee ? wines ? sugar ? State in general the chief productions of the Northwestern States ; the chief exports of the United States. What made New York State the greatest of the United States, and New York City the centre of commerce in the Western World ? To what distinguished governor is New York indebted for its greatness ?

3. Locate the following cities : *Denver, Santa Fé, Milwaukee, Louisville*, and *Toledo*. Name the States that touch the west side of the Mississippi.

4. Name the political divisions of South America and the capital of each. Locate the following cities : *Montevideo, Callao, Santiago, Pernambuco,* and *Caracas.*

5. Bound European Russia. Name its capital, three great rivers, and two mountain chains.

6. Through what waters would a vessel sail in going from Odessa to Riga with a cargo of wheat ?

7. What waters separate Great Britain from Ireland ? Name the largest four cities in Great Britain. State in round numbers the population of London.

8. What seas touch the east coast of Asia ? Name three great cities of Hindostan. What is the capital of Beloochistan ?

9. Bound Africa. What channel between Madagascar and the continent of Africa ? Through what waters would a ship sail in going from London to Calcutta by the shortest route ?

10. Locate the following cities : *Melbourne, Sydney,* and *Hobarttown.*

HISTORY.

1. From what monarchs did Columbus beg in vain for aid to enable him to discover a passage to the East Indies ? What sovereigns finally furnished him with an outfit ? With how many vessels did he sail ? With how many did he reach the West Indies, and with how many did he return ?

2. Who were the Puritans ? Why were they so called ? When and where did they land in America ? What States did they settle ? What Indian wars occurred in New England ? What form of government did the Puritans establish ?

3. Who settled Virginia, North and South Carolina ? What was the character of the first settlers ? When was South Carolina first settled ?

4. State the causes of the French and Indian War, and of the Revolutionary War. State the most important event in each of the following years : 1759, 1763, 1775, 1776, 1777.

5. What great American was mainly instrumental in securing French aid and in forming the treaty of alliance with

France ? Name four distinguished Frenchmen who aided America in the Revolution.

6. What is the Constitution of the United States ? What are the three great divisions of the government ? Which division imposes taxes ? Which enforces the laws ?

7. What States were introduced into the Union between 1789 and 1800 ? What was the Missouri Compromise ? Give its date.

8. What historical event is connected with each of the following names : Oliver H. Perry, Samuel F. B. Morse, De Witt Clinton, Mason and Slidell, and John Ericsson ?

9. What States passed ordinances of secession after the general election of 1860 ?

10. What Union officer commanded the land forces at Antietam ? at Gettysburg ? at Atlanta ? at Vicksburg ? and the naval forces at Mobile ?

SPELLING.

1. The marble *palace* of the *sovereign,* with its *arcades* and *corridors,* its *terraces* and courts, its lakes and groves and gardens, filled a *circuit* of ten miles ; its wide expanse of roof, profusely wrought in gold, rested upon hundreds of *pillars* of pure gold cunningly adorned in *arabesque* of azure to heighten the native richness of the yellow metal.

2. The rage of the *Portuguese* and the admiration of the *Spaniards* were alike blind. Neither nation was aware that the newly discovered land was inhabited by *savages.* The general impression prevailed that the *Bahama* Islands and the West Indies were only outlying portions of *Cathay.*

3. He *rode* to the *beach* on a *chestnut* horse which he *tied* to a branch of a *beech* tree. He waited for the *tide* to rise and then with *oars* he *rowed o'er* the river. He met a young *Dane* who would not *deign* to help him to load his boat with a *bale* of cotton. A stranger said he would go *bail* for his wages.

Philip.	Canada.
Hannibal.	Jamaica.

Matthew.   Havana.
Benjamin.   Savannah.
Ephraim.   Missouri.

College of the City of New York, 1890.

ARITHMETIC.

1. (*a*) What is a common fraction ?

(*b*) What is a decimal fraction ?

(*c*) What is ratio ?

(*d*) When are four numbers said to be in proportion ?

2. (*a*) Divide $1\frac{3}{8}$ by $\frac{1}{4}$.

(*b*) Reduce the following fractions to equivalent fractions having their least common denominator :

$$\frac{3}{10}, \quad \frac{2}{3} \text{ of } \frac{1}{7} \text{ of } \frac{2\frac{2}{7}}{3}, \quad \frac{1}{3} \text{ of } \frac{3}{8}.$$

(*c*) Add together the results obtained in (*b*).

3. (*a*) What fraction of $\frac{4}{5}$ is $\frac{1}{3}$?

(*b*) Find the value of $\frac{1}{14}$ of a mile in rods, yards, feet, and inches.

(*c*) Reduce $\frac{5}{80}$ to a decimal fraction.

4. What is the effect of dividing the denominator of a given common fraction by 4 ? Explain the reason of this.

5. (*a*) Write in decimal form the following :

Ten and ten hundredths ; nine millionths ; thirty thousandths ; thirteen hundred and forty-two hundredths.

(*b*) Add .003, 1.25, 20006.

(*c*) Divide .048 by 1600.

6. (*a*) Multiply .26 by .0035.

(*b*) Divide .006 by 10 by the shortest method.

(*c*) Explain the reason of this method.

7. If 4 men working 8 hours per day can mow a meadow in 3 days, how many men working 9 hours per day can mow a meadow three times as large in 4 days ?

8. A, B, and C entered into partnership for one year. A put in $5,000, B $6,000, and C $4,000. At the end of 6 months A withdrew $2,000 and C put in $8,000 more. The profits at the end of the year were $6,000. What was each man's share ?

9. A bought merchandise from B for $10,000 and gave his note for 6 months, without grace, with interest at 6%. Just when the note was due he sold the goods to C for $12,000, taking C's note at 3 months without interest, which his bank discounted for him at 6% the same day. After paying his note to B, how much money had he remaining ?

10. A drover bought a drove of 50 cattle for $2,000. He sold $\frac{1}{4}$ of them at a gain of 10% on the average price, and $\frac{1}{5}$ of them at a gain of 15%. Half of the remainder, however, were so injured in a railroad accident that he could only obtain $100 for them. For what price apiece must he sell the rest so that his total loss shall be $100 ?

ENGLISH.

1. Give the plural of court-martial, genus, spoonful ; the feminine of abbot, hero ; the superlative of ill, much, forth, far ; the past participle of begin, shake, drive, cleave, swim.

Change the following nouns into adjectives by means of suffixes : Gold, truth, boy, love, virtue, question.

2. State the class, mood, and tense of the verbs in the following sentences :

The dream was fled.

The Lord judge between thee and me.

I shall not look upon his like again.

Many acts that had been otherwise blamable were done by him.

3. Analyze the following sentences :

(a) Epictetus says: "Every matter has two handles, one of which will bear taking hold of, the other not."

(b) Art thou not content that thou hast done something conformable to thy nature, and dost thou seek to be paid for it, just as if the eye demanded a recompense for seeing ?

4. Correct the errors in the following sentences :

I expect it rained here yesterday.

The soil is adapted for wheat and corn.

We sorrow not as them that have no hope.

She is fairer, but not so amiable, as her sister.

No one ever sustained such mortifications as I have done to-day.

5. Write a simple sentence containing a participial and an infinitive phrase.

Write a compound sentence having two co-ordinate members, one of which shall be simple and the other complex.

GEOGRAPHY.

1. Draw a sketch map of the United States without State boundaries.

2. Locate thereon the sugar, cotton, tobacco, corn, wheat, and lumber belts, and the cities of San Francisco, Denver, Kansas City, St. Louis, Chicago, Duluth, Portland, Me., Baltimore, Charleston, New Orleans.

3. What is the most direct route from Edinburgh to Bombay ? Mention, in order, the countries and the waters traversed, and the ports at which the traveller lands or embarks.

4. What European peninsula projects northward from the continent ? What Asiatic peninsula westward ? Name two peninsulas in North America, two or three in Europe, three or four in Asia, which project southward.

5. Name the largest two countries in South America ; the smallest two. Which South American country has the longest coast line, absolutely ? Which the longest relatively to its area ?

6. The cities of Belgrade, Berlin, Leipsic, Stuttgart, Verona, and Warsaw are at nearly the same distance from Vienna. Draw a circle, put Vienna at the centre, and locate the six cities on the circumference. Draw another circle,

place Berne at the centre, and Cologne, Leghorn, Marseilles, Paris, and Venice on the circumference.

7. Draw the Mississippi and its branches, and give the approximate location of each State thereon.

8. What are air and ocean currents? How caused? State the name, location, and general direction of the most important ones; their influence upon the climate of continents.

9. Where is Queenstown? Through what channel, what sea, and to the mouth of what river does the steamer sail in continuing its trip from Queenstown to Liverpool? And in going from Liverpool to Glasgow, past what island, through what channel, up what firth and river?

10. Name and locate the largest five or six cities on the earth.

HISTORY.

1. Who were the earliest explorers of the Great Lakes and the Ohio and the Mississippi Rivers? Give names, dates, and some details. Also, what interesting relics or earthworks were found in that part of the country?

2. Give a brief account of the settlement of Rhode Island and New York. State, also, what occurred in New York between the years 1664 and 1674.

3. How did the French and Indian War differ, in its origin and results, from other colonial wars? Explain the final success of the English.

4. What were the causes of the Revolutionary War? Name three American victories and three defeats occurring between 1776 and 1780.

5. What large tracts of territory were granted to or purchased by the United States before 1805? What tracts have been secured since then, and in what way?

6. Name the Presidents who have served two terms, giving dates. Who was President during the 1812 War? Who during the Mexican War?

7. On what occasions did the slavery question greatly agitate the country ? Give full account of what took place in 1850.

8. State all that you know about Thomas Jefferson and Abraham Lincoln.

9. What questions were settled by the Civil War ? Give brief account of the closing military operations in 1865.

10. What is the present form of government in New York State, and when was it adopted ? Who were De Witt Clinton, William H. Seward, Millard Fillmore, S. F. B. Morse ?

SPELLING.

The mongoose is one of the *drollest* of animals, and he has no *fault* except *mischief* of a *personal* kind. But for *humorous surprises* he has *unequalled ingenuity*. If a *strange* lady entered, my mongoose *slipped* out of *sight,* crept up the hangings without a *rustle,* and when the lady was most *interested* in *explaining* her *business,* he *stretched* his long body and *introduced* a very cold nose *between* her *hair* and her *collar.*

Procession.	Seizure.	Synonymous.
Debtor.	Shriek.	Effervescent.
Address.	Professor.	Righteous.
Receipt.	Grievance.	Incessant.
Excitement.	Irritate.	Campaign.
Telegraphic.	Obey.	Emphasis.
Programme.	Criticism.	Scientific.
Wheelwright.	Acquit.	Exchange.
Bordeaux.	Rhode Island.	Raleigh.

Normal College.

ARITHMETIC.

1. When is a fraction said to be written in the vulgar form ? In the decimal form ? Write seven thousandths in both forms. Express 133⅓% decimally; also as a vulgar frac-

tion without reduction and as a vulgar fraction reduced to its lowest terms. State two ways of making a fraction smaller.

2. Find the result of the following operations :

$$60 - .012 + (\tfrac{4}{5} - \tfrac{3}{4}) \ .008.$$

3. A sold B goods for $394 at a loss of $1\tfrac{1}{4}\%$. B sold them to C at a profit of $1\tfrac{1}{4}\%$. Did they cost C more or less than A, and how much ?

4. All my money is invested at 7% and my annual income in $1,735. How much money have I ?

5. A merchant bought velvet at $5 a yard ; how much must he ask for it that he may make a discount of 10% from his asking price and still realize a profit of 15% ?

6. How much income annually will be obtained by investing $8,010 in 6% bonds selling at 89 ?

7. The interest of $500 at 6% for a certain time is $60 ; what principal will yield $75 interest in half the time at 8% ?

8. What is the cost of 2 tons, 15 cwt., 2 qr., 15 lbs. of hay at $21.50 a ton ? also at $1.12 a cwt. ?

ENGLISH.

I.

1. What is a part of speech ? Define *comparison*. Compare the words *little* and *much*. Name two adjectives that do not admit of comparison ; and give the reason.

2. What is an *abstract noun?* Write a compound sentence containing two abstract nouns in different clauses. What is a *collective noun?* Write two sentences each containing a collective noun, the one denoting *unity* and the other *plurality* of idea.

3. Write the principal parts of the verbs *burst, sit, set, lay, shoe.* What is a *participle?* How many kinds of participles are there ? Name them.

4. In words, as fashions, the same rule will hold,
   Alike fantastic if too new or old ;
   Be not the first by whom the new is tried,
   Nor yet the last to lay the old aside.—*Pope.*

(*a*) What kind of a sentence is the above stanza ? (*b*) Name the different clauses. (*c*) Name the subject and predicate of each clause. (*d*) State the kind of clause.

5. Parse *will hold, alike, new* (in the second line), *is tried* and *last.*

6. Parse *what* in each of the following lines :

We know *what* men we should honor. He does *what* he pleases.

What ! Does he fancy himself a Cæsar ?

II.

1. Convert the following into simple sentences : (*a*) He reported that the governor was dead. (*b*) The scholars who were educated by him became distinguished. (*c*) He told the troops that they must not fire on the enemy.

2. Define the word *invention.* Correct the sentence : " The joy is great which arises from the invention of truth." Define *vocation* and *avocation,* and construct a sentence containing both words correctly used.

3. Write a composition of not more than thirty and not less than twenty lines on ABRAHAM LINCOLN. [You will be marked for *punctuation,* use of *capitals,* the right use of *words* and grammatical construction of sentences.]

4. Punctuate and capitalize the following :

Two Gentlemen of the Country Lindesay and Kirkpatrick friends of Bruce were then in attendance on him seeing him pale bloody and in much agitation they eagerly inquired what was the Matter I doubt said Bruce that I have slain the red comyn do you leave such a matter in doubt said Kirkpatrick I will make sicker that is I will make certain accordingly he and his companion Lindesay rushed into the church and made certain with a Vengeance.

GEOGRAPHY.

1. What is a meridian ? What is the first meridian ? How many meridians are usually drawn on a terrestrial globe ? and why ? How many degrees are equal to one hour of time ?

2. The meridian of Alexandria (in Egypt) is 30° east and of New Orleans 90° west. On March 21st the sun rises at 6 o'clock in Alexandria, what is the time then at New Orleans ?

3. Bound Manhattan Island. In what direction are the following places from New York City : *Newark, Paterson, Long Island City, Manhattan Beach, Staten Island, Yonkers, Flushing, Trenton, Long Branch,* and *New Haven ?*

4. Name the four new States recently admitted into the Union. Bound Montana and state its capital.

5. Locate the following cities : *Paramaribo, Quito, Callao, Santiago, Bahia, Montevideo, Buenos Ayres, Aspinwall, Caracas,* and *Asuncion.*

6. Bound Great Britain. Locate the following cities : *London, Manchester, Liverpool, Glasgow, Edinburgh.* What is the most northerly point of Scotland ? The most southerly point of England ?

7. Name six mountain chains in Europe, and tell where they are situated. Name five islands in the Mediterranean in the order of their size.

8. Bound Afghanistan. Name two of its principal cities. What island south of British India ?

9. Through what waters would a ship pass in sailing from Liverpool to Calcutta by the shortest route ?

10. Name the divisions of Australia. Bound New South Wales and name its capital.

HISTORY.

1. How long did the Dutch hold New Amsterdam ? In whose reign was it captured by the English ? Who was the English military officer who captured it ? Who had the

better right to the territory, the Dutch or the English? State the reasons.

2. Describe the Conway Cabal. What was the most important battle of the Revolution? Why? Who were the respective commanders? Name the members of the committee who drafted the Declaration of Independence. What important military event virtually ended the Revolutionary War?

3. Name the three great departments of the United States government. Who is the chief officer of the national government? Who is the chief officer of the State government? Who is the chief officer of the city government? Who is the commander-in-chief of all the military and naval forces of the United States? State how a President of the United States is elected.

4. When and by whom were slaves introduced into the colony of Virginia? What celebrated act was passed by Congress in 1787? And what effect had it on the slavery question? When was the Compromise Bill passed? Explain this bill.

5. By what act was the Confederate war commenced? By what battle was it ended? Who was the great Secretary of the Treasury during this war? Name five battles in which General Grant was the chief commander. In which of these did he capture whole armies? What two Presidents were assassinated? What two died in office?

SPELLING.

In a cabinet *council* it was determined to *supersede* the French *minister's diplomatic* functions, deprive him of the consequent *privileges* and arrest his person; a message to Congress was in *preparation* at this *critical* juncture, when dispatches came from *Gouverneur* Morris announcing the minister's recall. . . . The *partisans* of France were now in the *ascendant*. It was scouted as *pusillanimous* any longer to hold terms with Great *Britain*. . . . The *populace* was *belligerent* and every means taken by the press and the democratic societies to exasperate this feeling. Washington, however, was too morally brave to be *clamored* out of his wise moderation by such taunts and *inflammatory* appeals.

The school was built on a lonely *site*.
Satan can *cite* scripture,
The *ascent* of the mountain was difficult.
The lord of the *manor* was a *baron*.

Accessible.	Gypsy.	Dorothy.
Defensible.	Apostasy.	Cynthia.
Allotted.	Cannibal.	Eustace.
Arable.	Cavalier.	Cornelius.
Typical.	Holiday.	Bartholomew.
Oracle.	Prelate.	Malaga.
Caravan.	Colossal.	Philippine.
Orifice.	Zephyr.	Ararat.
Elicit.	Rescind.	Caracas.
Cemetery.	Pigeon.	Sicily.

College of the City of New York, 1891.

1. (*a*) What is meant by the ratio of one quantity to another ?

(*b*) What is meant by the Greatest Common Divisor of several numbers ?   Give an example.

(*c*) What is meant by a minuend ? by a quotient ?

(*d*) When is a common fraction said to be in its lowest terms ?

2. (*a*) Reduce to its simplest form the following expression :

$$2\tfrac{1}{4} \times \tfrac{4}{5} \times \frac{2\tfrac{1}{2}}{\tfrac{3}{8}} \text{ of } 1\tfrac{4}{15}.$$

(*b*) Find the value of the following : $\tfrac{3}{4} + \tfrac{4}{5} - \tfrac{5}{8} + \tfrac{4}{5}$.

(*c*) Reduce $\tfrac{14}{11}$ to a decimal fraction.

3. (*a*) Find the value of $\frac{1}{140}$ of a mile in the lower denominations.

(*b*) What is the effect upon the value of a fraction if we multiply the denominator by three ?

(*c*) Explain the reason of the last answer.

4. (*a*) Write in decimal form the following :

Ten ten-thousandths.

One thousand and twenty-four ten-millionths.

Thirty-two and four thousandths.

(*b*) Multiply .0036 by 1.02.

(*c*) Divide 2.56 by .0016.

5. (*a*) If a cipher is added at the right of the decimal what effect has this on the value of the decimal ?

(*b*) Explain the reason of this.

6. (*a*) What part of $\frac{2}{3}$ is $\frac{4}{7}$?

(*b*) What is the easiest method of multiplying a decimal by 10 ?

(*c*) Reduce 20 square rods to the decimal of an acre.

7. If by selling a house for \$12,600 a builder gains $12\frac{1}{2}\%$, what per cent. would he have lost by selling it for \$8,400 ?·

8. A, B, and C began a partnership on January 1st. A put in \$10,000 ; B, \$6,000 ; and C, \$3,000. At the end of 6 months B put in \$4,000 more, but A withdrew \$2,000. At the end of the year they had on hand \$18,000 in cash and goods valued at \$12,000. At this time the property was divided and the firm dissolved, A taking all the goods as part of his share. How much *cash* did each of the three receive ?

9. A traveller going from one town to another walks $\frac{1}{3}$ of the distance on his first day's journey, $\frac{1}{4}$ of the remainder on the second day, 20 miles on the third day, and finds he has $\frac{4}{10}$ of the distance still to go. What is the distance ?

10. A dealer bought 1,200 barrels of flour at \$6 per barrel and shipped them to New York by railroad. An accident on the road destroyed $\frac{1}{3}$ of them. He sold the remainder at \$7.50 per barrel. His freight and cartage were \$312. He sued the railroad company and recovered some damages but

3

his legal expenses were $350.   At the close of the transaction he found he had made, over all expenses, just $138.   How much did he receive from the railroad company ?

ENGLISH.

1. Correct the errors in the following sentences and give the reason in each case for the correction:

(*a*) You cannot expect for a long time to write like he did.

(*b*) We were talking about our old friend who had sent me a flattering message, and I wondered did he mean it.

(*c*) Everybody nowadays publishes memoirs ; everybody has recollections which they think worthy of recording.

(*d*) Let there be but matter and opportunity offered and you shall see them quickly to revive again.

(*e*) The being abandoned by our friends is very deplorable.

2. Analyze the following sentence :

>   " High on a throne of royal state, that far
>   Outshone the wealth of Ormus and of Ind,
>   Or where the gorgeous East with richest hand
>   Showers on her kings Barbaric pearl and gold,
>   Satan exalted sat, by merit raised
>   To that bad eminence."

3. In how many and what ways do we denote comparison of adjectives ?   Give an example of each.

4. Give the principal parts of the following verbs.   If there are two forms of any principal part give both:

   Dive, Bereave, Cleave (*to split*), Swim, Abide, Thrive. Read, Quit, Swing, Breed.

5. Give the general rule for the correct use of " shall " and " will."

6. Write a letter to *James B. Murray*, asking a situation as clerk, stating your fitness for the place by education, age. and any other qualification you deem important. Sign the letter with the name *George Thomson* and be careful not to sign it with your own name.

GEOGRAPHY.

1. How much of the earth's surface is water ? On which ide of the equator is most of the water ? Name some of the argest lakes and the largest sheet of fresh water on the arth.

2. One-half of the land is divided among five powers : ame them. Tell of each where its possessions lie.

3. Name the sea between Africa and Europe, the sea beween Africa and Arabia, the channel between Africa and Iadagascar, the large gulf which indents the western coast f Africa. In what part of Africa is Abyssinia ? Cape Colny ? Egypt ? Liberia ? Morocco ? the Congo Free State ?

4. What mountains must one cross in going from Virginia o Kentucky ? from Dakota to Oregon ? from the Argentine Republic to Chili ? from Spain to France ? from Hindostan o China ?

5. In what European country is Antwerp ? Athens ? Bristol ? Leipzig ? Luzerne ? Marseilles ? Moscow ? Na-les ? Seville ? Utrecht ?

6. Draw a map of New England (fairly covering half the heet of paper) showing the State borders ; the Connecticut nd the Merrimac ; Lake Champlain and Narragansett Bay ; Boston, Burlington, Hartford, New Haven, Portland, and 'rovidence. Write the names (in reasonable abbreviation).

7. What is the climate of California ? What is the haracter of its vegetation ? What are, therefore, the chief ndustries of the State ?

8. Tell what you know of glaciers and of icebergs.

HISTORY.

1. At the outbreak of our Revolutionary War what four ifferent groups of European settlers were living in North America ? Locate them, and give the population of the argest groups at the time.

2. What powers have had possession of New York City

since its first settlement? and explain when and why it passed from the control of one to another.

3. Name the three most important wars fought on this continent, and state the cause and result of the first one.

4. Give the history of the Stamp Act. What other acts of taxation did the colonists resist?

5. The battles of Long Island and Trenton : describe each briefly and estimate their importance as Revolutionary events.

6. When and under what circumstances were Louisiana, California, and Florida acquired by the United States?

7. State concisely for what the following men have been distinguished in our history : Thomas MacDonough, Anthony Wayne, "Stonewall" Jackson, Aaron Burr, John C. Fremont, Wendell Phillips, Winfield Scott, Daniel Morgan, Daniel Webster, John Adams.

8. Why did the Southern States secede from the Union in 1860–61? What two great victories turned the tide of the war in favor of the North?

9. What led to the adoption of the Federal Constitution? When and where adopted, and what do you understand by it?

10. Name the Presidents who served two terms, giving dates. Who was President when John Brown was executed? Who when the first Atlantic cable was laid?

SPELLING.

1. If the *jealousy* of the *Parliament* and of the *nation* made it *impossible* for the king to *maintain* a *formidable* standing army, no *similar impediment prevented* him from making England the first of *maritime* powers. (Macaulay.)

2. For many days the *vessel* was *tossed* about and all on board were *filled* with *apprehensions*, and no little *indignation against* the *author* of their *calamities*. (Prescott.)

3. The second was an *inquiry* how it could be *rendered practicable* to *discuss political* matters in future—a *proceeding* now impossible, in *consequence* of the *perverseness* and

arrogance of *certain functionaries*, and one which whenever *attempted* always led to the same *inevitable* result.   (Motley.)

Normal College.

ARITHMETIC.

1. Define the following terms employed in arithmetic : *Quantity, number, abstract number, multiplication, proportion.*

Explain the reason for multiplying the second and third terms together and dividing by the first term in solving an example in simple proportion.

2. $\dfrac{\frac{3}{4}\text{ of }1\frac{1}{2}}{\frac{1}{11}\text{ of }5\frac{1}{2}}$ is what part of $\dfrac{\frac{3}{4}\text{ of }3\frac{3}{4}}{\frac{1}{4}\text{ of }5\frac{1}{4}}$?

3. Columbus is 83° 3′ west longitude, and when it is 37 min. 33 sec. past 1 P.M. it is 11 o'clock A.M. in San Francisco. What is the longitude of the latter city ?

4. Divide thirty-two hundred-millionths by sixty-four ten-thousandths.

5. A, B, and C gained by speculation $11,480, of which A's share was twice as much as C's, and B's five times as much as C's.   How much did each gain ?

6. A man owes $600, of which one-third is to be paid in one year and the remainder in two years.   What is the present value, money worth 6% ?

7. I bought a watch for $120 and set such a price on it that after falling $12 I still made 15% on the purchase. What per cent. did I abate from the asking price ?

8. A pole was broken 52 feet from the bottom and fell so that the end struck 39 feet from the foot.   Required the length of the pole.

9. Extract the cube root of $\frac{343}{34}$ to five places of decimals.

10. Sold a horse so that $\frac{1}{4}$ of the gain equalled $\frac{3}{15}$ of the cost.   What was the gain per cent. ?

ENGLISH.

1. Name five different kinds of nouns.

(a) In the sentence,

"Oh, how this spring of love resembleth
The uncertain glory of an April day,"

name the nouns and state the kind of each.

(b) What part of speech is *how?* What does it modify?

(c) What is case? Name the cases.

(d) In the sentence,

"The supplies having reached us the army began its march," name the nouns and state the kind and case of each.

2. Name four kinds of verbs in regard to their *form.*

(a) Name four kinds of verbs in regard to their *signification.*

(b) In the sentence,

"Home-keeping youths have ever homely wits," state what kind of a verb *have* is according to its *form* and also according to its *signification.*

(c) In the sentence,

"Beware of entering into a quarrel," parse *beware* and *entering.*

(d) In the sentence,

"He was laughed at," explain the verb in regard to its *signification.*

3. Write eight auxiliary verbs.

(a) Write the potential mood, pluperfect tense of the verb *to write.*

(b) What kind of a verb is *cleave?* Write its principal parts.

(c) In the sentence,

"I can always buy such books as I want," parse *as.*

4. Name seven different kinds of clauses.

(a) Give an example of a subject clause.

(b) In the sentence,

"As I told thee before, I am subject to a tyrant, a sorcerer that by his cunning hath cheated me of the island," parse the words *thee, subject, that.*

(*c*) What kind of sentence is it? Name each clause and its kind.

5. Write a noun clause in apposition to a noun used as subject of a sentence.

(*a*) Write a compound sentence consisting of two co-ordinate clauses, each of which is complex with the dependent clause adjective in the first and adverbial in the second.

II.

1. In five sentences introduce the following words : *Object, concord, dissent, involve,* and *prospect.*

2. By substitution of other prefixes change these words to their opposite meanings in five other sentences.

3. Explain the difference between *courage* and *bravery* in a compound sentence with two co-ordinate clauses, using the word *but* as the connective.

4. Write in three paragraphs of not less than six nor more than ten lines each what you consider the principal qualities of a good student, of a good teacher, and the main object of education.

5. Define paragraph. Name the punctuation points which may be made at the end of a sentence. When would you use a comma and when a semicolon ? Construct a sentence in which you employ the comma, the semicolon, the dash, and the period. Name all the kinds of words that are commenced with capital letters.

6. Write a letter to the Governor of the State of New York, requesting him to use his influence to establish civil service reform *in the appointment* of all teachers.

[The letter must not exceed fifteen lines. *Credit will be given for arrangement, punctuation, the right use of words, and the correct construction of sentences.* The mark for executive ability will be given on this letter.]

GEOGRAPHY.

1. What is the greatest latitude that any place can have ?
Where has a place no latitude ?
What is the greatest longitude a place can have ?
Name the southern boundary of the Torrid Zone.
Mention two things that determine climate.

2. Bound the State of New York.
Name five of its cities as nearly as you can in the order of their size.
What is the largest city on Long Island ?
Locate Sag Harbor, Geneva, Oswego, Elmira, and Utica.
State as nearly as you can in round numbers the population of New York City, and also of New York State.

3. Name the capitals of West Virginia, South Dakota, Texas, Iowa, and North Carolina.
Name five rivers of the United States that empty themselves into the Atlantic Ocean.
Mention two great railroad lines by which you could travel from New York to Buffalo.

4. Bound Great Britain.
Write the capitals of England, Scotland, and Ireland, and the rivers on which they are situated.
Locate Liverpool, Bristol, Glasgow, Belfast, and Oxford.
Name four rivers of France.
Locate the following islands : Corfu, Elba and Jersey.

5. Locate the following cities of Asia : Bombay, Lassa, Ispahan, Mecca, Smyrna, Madras, Nankin, Calcutta, and Singapore.
Name three great rivers of Asia that empty themselves into the Arctic Ocean.
Locate the following cities of South America: Buenos Ayres, Bahia, and Lima.

HISTORY.

1. Who discovered and explored the St. Lawrence River ?
Who discovered the Mississippi River ? Who subsequently

explored it ?   What two nations claimed the valleys of the
Ohio and the Mississippi ?   State the claim of each.   What
was the result of the French and Indian war ?   What English general captured the citadel of Louisburg ?

2. Describe briefly the route of Burgoyne in his invasion
of New York.   What battles were fought ?   Who was the
American commander ?   What American officers' distinguished themselves in this campaign ?   What great American was chiefly instrumental in forming treaties of alliance
with France and other European countries ?

3. Give a brief explanation of the government of the
United States, stating, first, the form of government ; second,
the three great departments of the government ; third, the
powers and duties of each department ; and fourth, the principal officer in each department.

4. Who was President during the war of 1812–15 ?   Who
gained the great naval victory on Lake Erie ?   Who was
President when the Missouri Compromise Bill was passed ?
Explain this bill.   Who was President during the Mexican
War ?   What territory was acquired at the end of this War ?

5. There were two great victories gained in July, 1863 :
name them.   Who commanded the Union army in the East
—who in the West ?   What three important cities did Sherman capture in his celebrated march to the sea ?   What was
the grand result of the great Civil War ?

SPELLING.

The *expedition* which sailed from Halifax against *Louisburg,* under the command of *Brigadier*-General *Amherst,*
consisted of twenty ships of the line, *eighteen frigates,* and
an army of fourteen thousand men.   After a *siege* of a few
days the *fortress* was *surrendered.*   At the same time Cape
Breton fell into the hands of the *British.*

Colonel *Bradstreet solicited* and obtained *permission* to
surprise and *seize* Fort Frontenac at the northwest outlet of
Lake Ontario.   With three thousand *soldiers* he moved with

celerity, took the fort, and with it nine armed vessels, sixty cannon, *sixteen mortars*, and a great quantity of *ammunition*.

The *campaign* closed with honor to the *colonies*. Preparation was made for the greater *achievements* of 1759. A treaty of peace and *friendship* was made with the Indians *inhabiting* the lands between the *Appalachian* Mountains, the *Alléghanies*, and the lakes.

Absinthe.	Jocund.	Raillery,
Bacchanal.	Kangaroo.	Scythian.
Calcimine,	Labyrinth.	Taciturnity.
Daguerreotype.	Lorraine.	Utility.
Edible.	Maceration.	Vitriol.
Farinaceous.	Nutritious.	Thibet.
Gibbeting.	Ocular.	Galilee.
Hypnotize.	Pelican.	Edinburgh.
Immutable.	Quiescence.	Grenada.

College of the City of New York, 1892.

ARITHMETIC.

1. (*a*) What is meant by a decimal fraction ?

   (*b*) Define a minuend ; a multiplicand ; a quotient.

   (*c*) In every common fraction what is shown by the denominator ? What by the numerator ?

2. (*a*) Reduce to its simplest from the following expression :

$$\frac{3\frac{1}{4}}{4\frac{1}{8}} \text{of} \frac{12}{7} \times \frac{7}{3}.$$

   (*b*) Reduce the following fractions to their *least* common denominator : $\frac{3}{4}, \frac{2}{9}, \frac{2}{3}$ of $\frac{15}{16}.$

   (*c*) Find the value of $\frac{1}{4}$ of $\frac{3}{8} + \frac{1}{4} - \frac{1}{11}.$

3. (*a*) What part of $\frac{5}{8}$ is $\frac{3}{4}$?

   (*b*) Reduce $\frac{3}{800}$ to a decimal fraction.

   (*c*) Multiply .05 by 3.2.

4. (*a*) If the numerator of a common fraction is divided by 3, what is the effect upon the value of the fraction ?

(*b*) If the denominator is divided by 3, what is the effect upon the value of the fraction ?

(*c*) Explain the reason of this last result.

5. (*a*) Write in decimal form : Ninety millionths; thirty ten thousandths ; ten, and twenty-five thousandths.

(*b*) Divide .064 by .000016.

(*c*) Add .003, 12.06, 1.1.

(*d*) Subtract 2.3 from 4.006.

6. (*a*) What is the effect of the value of a decimal of moving the decimal point two places to the right ?

(*b*) Explain the reason of this.

(*c*) In multiplication of two decimals how many decimal places are to be pointed off in the product ?

(*d*) Explain the reason of this rule.

7. How much is 5⅘ tons of coal worth, if 17¾ tons are worth $100 ?

8. A person expended 16% of all he was worth in buying 20% of the stock of a Mining Company. If the entire stock of the company sold for $160,000, what must the person have been worth ?

9. Four men undertook to do a piece of work in 18 days and worked at it 6 hours a day for 10 days, when they found they had finished only ¼ of it. How many *more* men did they have to engage in order to finish the job by the time agreed upon, provided they all worked thereafter for 10 hours each day ?

10. A provision merchant bought 100 barrels of apples at a farm-house at $1 per barrel, and paid 5 cents per barrel to have them taken to the railroad station. Then he paid $50 freight on them to New York and $20 cartage in the city. They were sold at once for $3 per barrel, but the commission merchant charged him 10% commission on the sale. Also when some of the barrels were opened the apples were found to be damaged and he had to repay the purchasers $20 on account of this. How much did he gain in all ?

ENGLISH.

1. We frequently hear it said : "*That is bad grammar.*" Explain what is meant by "bad grammar."

2. Why is it considered wrong to say (*a*) "*most perfect,*" (*b*) "*most circular,*" (*c*) "*supremest,*" (*d*) "*chiefest,*" (*e*) "*most infinite?*"

3. Correct the errors in the following sentences and give a reason or rule for each correction :

(*a*) That awkward country boy learns faster than us all.

(*b*) There is nothing to prevent him going.

(*c*) My mother gave me three tea-spoonsful of the medicine.

(*d*) I asked the carpenter to lend me his two feet rule.

(*e*) His teacher learns her boys better than our teacher learns us.

(*f*) I called but you was not at home.

(*g*) I says to him : "Run away as fast you can."

(*h*) I will try and catch the horse.

(*i*) The next New Year's day I shall be at school three years.

(*j*) I know that he cannot do this like I did it.

4. What are tenses and moods in Grammar? Give the first person plural of the tenses in the different moods of the active verb "strike."

5. Why do we use pronouns? Show the advantage gained by the use of "he" and "which" in constructing one sentence out of the following :

"Cæsar crossed the Rubicon. The Rubicon is a river not far from Rome. Cæsar found no opposition on entering Rome."

N. B.—Substitute another word for the second "Rome."

6. Construct a sentence about George Washington (*a*) with an object clause ; (*b*) also one with a subject clause ; (*c*) also one with a subject infinitive phrase. Underline each clause and the phrase.

7. Turn this poetry into prose.

(a) " My heart leaps up when I behold

(b) A rainbow in the sky ;

(c) So was it when my life began,

(d) So is it now I am a man,

(e) So be it when I shall grow old,

(f) Or let me die ! "

8. In the foregoing selection parse the word "*when*" in line (a) ; the word "*was*" in line (c) ; the word "be" in line (e) ; and the words " *let* " and " *die* " in line (f).

9. Analyze the following sentence :

" The bliss of man,—could man that blessing find—

Is not to act or think beyond mankind."

10. Write a composition of not less than 75 words in length on one of the following subjects :

(a) " The Chicago Fair."

(b) " Is a cable-road better than a horse-railroad ? "

(c) " Why is rapid transit desirable ? "

(d) " Describe Riverside Drive."

(e) " Describe the Brooklyn Bridge."

(f) " Why do I (you) seek admission to college ? "

Notice that the punctuation, capitals, grammar, and good sense of your composition will be carefully criticised, and be careful to write the composition on a separate sheet.

GEOGRAPHY.

1. What is the shape of the earth ? What two constant motions has it ? What do they cause ?

2. Name the zones. What is the extent of each ? What determines this extent ?

3. Sketch a map of the State of New York (covering one-half the sheet of paper). Show and name the States and waters bordering on it, its rivers, mountains, valleys, islands, and cities.

4. What geographical advantages are possessed by the cities of New York, Boston, Chicago, and San Francisco ?

5. Name the chief articles of commerce between the United States and France; Australia; China; Brazil; Malaysia.

6. In what European country and on what water is Havre; Lisbon; Messina; Copenhagen; St. Petersburg; London; The Hague; Hammerfest; Constantinople; Stockholm?

7. Through what waters and by what countries would you pass in sailing from San Francisco to New York, stopping on the way at Melbourne, Aden, and Liverpool?

8. Name the highest mountain and the longest river in North America; in South America; in Europe; in Asia; in Africa; in Australia.

9. What is a delta? How is it formed? Name and locate the great deltas.

10. Sketch a map of the British Islands. Indicate the chief divisions of land and water represented thereon.

HISTORY.

1. Describe the voyages of Columbus, and give a brief sketch of his life.

2. Give the history of New Netherlands under its last Dutch Governor. Who was the first American Governor of New York?

3. What was King Philip's war? Also, Queen Anne's war? Give main facts, dates, etc.

4. Why did the colonists refuse to pay a tax on tea? Follow events thereafter to the 19th of April, 1775.

5. Give an account of the campaign that ended in Burgoyne's surrender. Why was that event of special importance to the American cause?

6. What territory did the United States acquire in 1787? and how? When and how was Texas acquired?

7. Give the leading events of Madison's and Jackson's administrations.

8. Why did the Southern States secede in 1861? Why cannot slavery be revived?

9. Give an account of Lee's invasion of Pennsylvania in 1863. Name three great defeats the North sustained during the war.

10. Name the Presidents in order from Monroe to Grant. Under which one was Daniel Webster Secretary of State? Who was President when California was admitted into the Union?

SPELLING.

The great *historic systems* of writing are of such *immense antiquity* that their history has to be explained to a great extent by the aid of *conjecture* and *analogy*. Hence the *rudimentary* forms of *picture* writing which we find among the less *cultured* races are of *considerable* interest and value, *inasmuch* as they throw light on the *earlier* stages of the *development* of *graphic* symbols. (Isaac Taylor.)

Austria at first *ostensibly favored* the *Poles*. The *Vienna* and *St. Petersburg Cabinets* were at that time far from *friendly*. Austria *suspected* and feared the *Russian* plots to excite *rebellion* in Turkey, which could not but be *prejudicial* to her interests. Russia, the foremost *advocate* of *passive* and slavish *obedience*, *scruples* not, when it *suits* her plans, to *foment* rebellion among her *neighbors*. *Bismarck* had *endeavored* to draw Austria to the side of Russia. The *treaty* with Russia before *mentioned* made the *question* a *European* one. (Dyer.)

Normal College.

ARITHMETIC.

1. (*a*) Define prime number.

(*b*) When is one number said to be prime to another?

(*c*) Define the least common multiple and the greatest common divisor of a number.

(*d*) Define commercial or bank discount.

2. Simplify $\dfrac{1\frac{3}{8} - 5\frac{1}{4} \times \frac{4}{13} - \frac{3}{15}}{\frac{1}{4} + \frac{1}{4} - 1\frac{3}{4}}.$

3. Simplify $\dfrac{.321 \times .321 - .179 \times .179}{.321 - .179}$ of 5.

4. Divide 3,432 into 3 parts proportional to 3, 4, and 5.

5. At 3 cents a pound how many tons of iron can be bought for $396.18 ?

6. If 50 men can build 50 rods of wall in 75 days, how many men will be required to build 80 rods of wall $\frac{2}{3}$ as thick and $\frac{4}{5}$ as high in 40 days ?

7. A lawyer having a debt of $1,536 to collect, compromises for 95%. What is his commission at $4\frac{1}{2}$% and what does he remit to his employer ?

8. A broker bought for me 76 shares of bank stock (par value of each share $50) at $47\frac{1}{4}$. What did the stock cost me, the brokerage being $\frac{1}{4}$% ?

9. Two vessels sailed from the same port, one sails north 3 miles an hour, the other west 4 miles an hour. How far are they apart in two days ?

10. Extract the cube root of 633839.779.

ENGLISH.

I.

" My father loved Sir Rowland as his soul,
    And all the world was of my father's mind;
    Had I before known this young man his son
    I should have given him tears unto entreaties,
    Ere he should thus have ventured."

1. (a) What kind of a sentence is the above quotation ?

(b) Name the first clause and state the kind of clause.

(c) Name the second clause and state the kind of clause.

(d) Name the third clause and state the kind of clause.

(e) Name all the subjects and predicates from " My " to " ventured."

2. Parse *soul, all, son, before, ere.* State the mood and tense of *ventured.*

3. Nobody else was just there ; parse *else* and *just.*
Write sentences in which the word *but* is correctly used as a
noun, as a conjunction, as a preposition, and as an adverb.

4. Construct a compound sentence with two co-ordinate
clauses, the first being a complex and the second a compound
clause.

Write a sentence containing an adverbial clause ; a sentence
containing an adjective clause.

5. Define *declension, conjugation, syntax, mood,* and *tense.*

II.

1. Write a letter about the Normal College. Where situated ? What kind of building ? Handsome, large, well-
lighted, cheerful ? How you reach it from your residence ?
Describe the room in which you are writing your examination.

[*Credit will be given for arrangement, proper division into
paragraphs, punctuation right use of words, and capitals and
correct construction of sentences.*]

2. What is the meaning of anti-slavery ? Give the word
which is the opposite of anti-slavery, and use both words in a
single sentence. Give another word beginning with *anti.*
Define antecedent and state how the word is used in grammar.

3. Define accede, intercede, proceed, recede, and supersede
and construct sentences containing each word.

4. What is the most important word in a sentence ? Define subject, predicate, and object. By what arrangement
of words is clearness of expression most readily secured ?

5. Punctuate and capitalize the following :

The autograph album prepared by a committee of the
press club for exhibition and sale at the actors fund fair is
richly bound with gold trimmed covers and a quaint illus-
trated title page exclusive of cartoon illustrations by well
known artists the book contains sixty pages each bearing a
sentiment respecting the stage personally inscribed by some
american celebrity in journalism or general literature.

William D. Howells contributes a quatrain as follows
        The wit supreme and sovereign sage
        has told us all the worlds a stage
        The curtain on his scene up-furled
        shows us the stage is all the world.

GEOGRAPHY.

1. (a) Write the cause of the change of the seasons.

(b) How many degrees from the North Pole to the Tropic of Capricorn ?

(c) What is the length of a degree at the Equator in geographical miles ?   In statute miles ?

2. (a) In what part of the world will you find the antipodes of New York ?

(b) What State of the United States was once an independent republic ?

(c) To what government is the Holy Land now subject ?

3. (a) Name in order of size the largest five cities of the United States.

(b) Where is Harvard University, Yale College, Cornell University, Vassar College ?

(c) Locate the following cities : Venice, Copenhagen, Dantzic, Odessa, Carthagena.

4. (a) Bound Behring Sea.   What valuable article of commerce is obtained in that region ?

(b) Where is the Bay of Fundy and for what is it noted?

(c) Name the principal products of Brazil and of the Argentine Confederation.

5. (a) Name two important islands belonging to the State of New York.

(b) What two large islands southeast of Asia are crossed by the Equator ?

(c) Name ten seas bordering on Asia.

HISTORY.

1. (a) By what people was America discovered prior to Columbus, and what part of the American continent did they touch ?

(*b*) Relate the history of Hudson and his voyages.

(*c*) When and where was the first English settlement made in America.

2. (*a*) Name the three wars prior to the French and Indian War caused by troubles in Europe.

(*b*) Write a brief account of the Salem witchcraft.

(*c*) What languages were spoken in New York in the latter part of the seventeenth century ?

3. (*a*) What action did the Continental Congress of 1774 take, and what action was taken by the second Continental Congress.in 1775 ?

(*b*) Give a brief account of the battle of Long Island.

(*c*) What great naval victory was gained by Paul Jones ?

(*d*) Name five noted statesmen of the Revolutionary period.

(*e*) Name the captors of Major André and state how they were rewarded.

4. (*a*) Where was the seat of government when Washington was inaugurated ?

(*b*) What is meant by the so-called " era of good feeling " and who was President at the time ?

(*c*) Write a short sketch of Mr. Lincoln's life previous to his becoming President.

5. (*a*) Name the States that seceded in 1861.

(*b*) In what city was the Confederate government first established and to what city was it subsequently removed ?

(*c*) Give a brief account of the battle of Gettysburg.

SPELLING.

THOMAS CAMPBELL.

To the *suggestion* and *eloquent advocacy* of this *distinguished* man the London *University* is said to have owed its *origin*.

" The *Pleasures* of Hope " is a *splendid* poem. Its *polish* is *exquisite*, its topics *felicitously* chosen, and its *illustration natural* and *beautiful*. He lifts you up to an *exceedingly* high *mountain,* and you see all nature in her *loveliness,* and man in the truth of his *character,* with hope *irradiating, cheering* and. *sustaining* him in the *numerous* ills of life. " *Gertrude* of *Wyoming* " is *preferred* by some readers even to his " *Pleasures* of Hope " It is a sad tale, told with *tenderness* as well as *genius.* But if these had never been written, his songs would have given him claims as a first-rate poet.

Censure.	Incense.	Susceptible.
Defamation.	Hygiene.	Morrisania.
Degradation.	Homicide.	Abyssinia.
Irritate.	Heresy.	Christiana.
Irascible.	Galaxy.	Finisterre.
Inflammation.	Feudal.	Ryswick.
Illicit.	Sacrilegious.	

College of the City of New York, 1893.

ARITHMETIC.

1. (*a*) What is a minuend ?

(*b*) What is a quotient ?

(*c*) Give the rule for the division of one common fraction by another.

(*d*) What is discount ?

2. Find the value of

(*a*) $\frac{\frac{3}{4}}{2\frac{1}{4}}$ of $\frac{1}{7}$ of $2\frac{1}{2} + \frac{3}{4}$.

(*b*) Add $\frac{3}{4}$ of $\frac{2}{3}$, $\frac{3}{8}$, $\frac{1}{7}$ of $\frac{11}{16}$.

3. (*a*) Find the value of $\frac{8}{35}$ Ton in whole numbers of lower denominations.

(*b*) If the numerator and denominator of a common fraction be divided by the same number, what effect is produced upon the value of the fraction ?

(*c*) Explain the reason of this.

4. (*a*) Write in decimal form : nine millionths ; three hundred ten thousandths ; ten thousand and ten millionths.

(*b*) Divide .096 by 3.2.

(*c*) Add 100.216, 3.0046, 3126.04.

5. (*a*) When two decimals are multiplied together, how many decimal places must be pointed off in the product ?

(*b*) Explain the reason of this rule.

6. What capital must be invested in 4% bonds bought at 15% premium in order to yield an income of $7,500 ?

7. A garrison had provisions enough for 1,800 men for six months, but having sent away a detachment, the provisions lasted ten months. How many men were sent away ?

8. A merchant had his note for $10,000 discounted at a bank for six months, without grace, at 6%. With the proceeds he bought goods, and sold ⅘ of them during the six months at a profit of 15%, and then closed out the remainder for $1,200 cash. When he had paid his note at the bank how much had he left ?

9. Two brothers each inherited at the same time $4,000. One put his money in savings banks, where it received 4% compound interest each year. The other, during the first year, lost $100 by investments and spent $200 in travelling. Then he invested all he had left in a business venture and, at the end of two years more, received back his money with 20% profit. Which of the brothers had then the more money, and how much more ?

10. A and B and C can together do a piece of work in 5 days. A alone can do it in 20 days ; B alone can do it in 30 days. In what time can it be done by B and C working together ?

ENGLISH.

1. Write sentences of not less than twenty words, in each of which sentences the word *that* is used as a different part of speech.

2. Combine these eight sentences into *one sentence* :

"An owl lived in a tree. He was a white owl. He was large. He lived in the hollow of the tree. The tree was old

4. Give the principal events and measures leading to the outbreak of the American Revolution—1765 to 1775.

5. Describe the final campaign of the Revolutionary War, and state the terms of the treaty of peace with Great Britain.

6. Name the Presidents down to the close of the War of 1812. What advantages did the United States secure through that war ?

7. Give an account of the administrations of Presidents Jackson and Polk.

8. State all you know respecting the following public men . in our history :—Alexander Hamilton, Henry Clay, De Witt Clinton, Nathaniel Greene, Admiral Farragut.

9. Describe the political situation in 1860–61, showing what influences and causes brought about the Civil War.

10. (*a*) What form of government do we have in this State to-day, and what was the form in colonial times ?

(*b*) What tie binds us to the other States ?

(*c*) Why cannot slavery be revived in the United States ?

Spelling.

Hundreds of *broad-headed, short-stemmed, wide-branched* oaks, which had *witnessed* perhaps the *stately* march of the Roman *soldiery,* flung their *gnarled* arms over a thick carpet of the most *delicious greensward* ; in some places they were *intermingled* with *beeches, hollies,* and *copsewood* of various *descriptions,* so closely as *totally* to *intercept* the level beams of the *sinking* sun ; in others they *receded* from each other, forming those long, *sweeping vistas,* in the *intricacy* of which the eye *delights* to lose itself, while *imagination considers* them as the paths to yet wilder scenes of *sylvan solitude.*

Here the red *rays* of the sun shot a broken and *discolored* light, that *partially* hung upon the *shattered boughs* and *mossy* trunks of the trees, and there they *illuminated* in *brilliant patches* the *portions* of turf to which they made their way.

southeast of Hindoostan, that east of Africa, that south of Argentina.

3. Name the three States on the Pacific, the five on the Gulf, the two on Chesapeake Bay, the two on Delaware Bay, the eight on the Lakes.

4. Name the body of water into which the Danube flows, the Des Moines, the Ganges, the Mackenzie, the Nile, the Platte, the Po, the Thames, the Wabash, the Yukon.

5. Through what strait must a ship pass on the voyage from Marseilles to Havre? from Venice to Genoa? from Constantinople to Naples? from Hull to Stockholm?

6. Name the capital of Persia, of Italy, of Belgium, of Portugal, of Peru, of Venezuela, of Connecticut, of Tennessee, of Kansas, of Canada.

7. Name the highest point on the Earth, in North America, in the United States east of the Mississippi, in Europe; and state, as nearly as you can, the height and location of each (the range to which it belongs).

8. What is a Geyser? a Delta? a Watershed? a River basin, or valley? a Reef?

9. When it is noon at Washington it is midnight at Bangkok; how many degrees east of Washington is Bangkok? Name some portion of the British Empire where it is midsummer when it is midwinter in England.

10. Which are the most valuable animals of the Arctic regions? Which animals and plants (trees) are peculiar to the Tropical regions?

HISTORY.

1. Name the European nations that secured a foothold in America at any time before 1775. What parts did each claim?

2. Describe the different kinds of English colonial government, and give an example of each.

3. Give an account of King Philip's War; also, of the French and Indian War, including its cause, events and result.

and rotten. It was an oak-tree. It stood on the top of the hill. The hill was back of our house."

3. Name the different classes of pronouns, and give examples of each class.

4. When is it correct to say : " The Committee *is* in session to-day," and when is it correct to say : "The Committee *are* in session to-day ?"

5. Copy the following sentences, *correcting errors :*

We shall have a holiday upon Monday.

Divide this between the three girls.

On what train did you come in on ?

Of these three kings, the latter was the wisest.

If we do wrong we will be punished.

6. Illustrate by examples the difference between simple, compound, and complex sentences.

7. What tenses are formed **by the** use of auxiliaries ? Use the verb *strike* to show this.

8. Analyze the following, and notice that a diagram is greatly to be preferred, provided it is neatly and carefully made.

" *When reposing* that *night* on my pallet of straw,

By the wolf-scaring fagot *that* guarded the slain,

At the dead of the night a sweet vision I saw,

And thrice *ere* the morning 1 dreamt it again."

9. Parse the words italicized in the foregoing sentence.

10. Write a composition of not less than one hundred words about "Thomas Jefferson," or "Abraham Lincoln," or the recent "Naval Review at New York." Be careful to write this on a separate sheet.

GEOGRAPHY.

1. Name the countries which border upon the Russian Empire.

2. Name the island south of Florida, that east of Quebec, that east of Greenland, that north of Norway, that east of Corea, that north of Java, that south of Australia, that

Normal College.

ARITHMETIC.

1. What is the value of a fraction multiplied by its denominator? What is the effect of removing the decimal point one place to the left? one place to the right? Write a promissory note. Define the terms *maker, payee* and *holder*.

2. Express by Roman notation 81,963.

3. Find the value of $\left(\dfrac{4\frac{4}{5}}{8\frac{1}{10}} \text{ of } \dfrac{3}{7\frac{1}{2}}\right)$ divided by $\frac{6}{11}$.

4. Divide 375 by .75 and .75 by 375 and find the sum and difference of the quotients.

5. $3,675 was offered to a man for his house, or $4,235 in three years without interest. He accepted the latter offer. Did he gain or lose, and how much, money being worth 7%?

6. A gentleman owns stock in a manufactory which pays annually 9%. He receives quarterly $324. What sum has he invested?

7. Two partners engaged in business. One furnished ⅔ of the whole capital; and the other $4,000. They gained in trade 20% on their capital, but lost $500 from bad debts. What was each partner's share of the net gain?

8. 600 yards of cloth ⅚ yards wide being required to make suits for 250 soldiers, how much cloth ⅞ yards wide will be needed to make suits for 1,200 men?

9. A general has an army of 226,576 men. How many must he place rank and file to form them into a square?

10. Find the cube root of 3 to three decimal places.

ENGLISH.

I.

1. Give the rules for the formation of the plurals of nouns and illustrate each rule by an example. Define case. Tell how case is expressed.

2. In how many ways are adjectives compared? Give an example of each. Name three adjectives that do not admit of comparison and assign the reason. Write the second future tense (known also as the future perfect) indicative mood, in the first person singular of raise, rise, lay, lie, set.

3. Correct the following and state the reasons—

(*a*) I am one of those who cannot describe what I feel.

(*b*) I had hoped never to have witnessed the like again.

(*c*) Nor eye, nor listening ear, an object find.

(*d*) This injury his been done me by my friend, he whom I treated like a brother.

(*e*) What is the use of you talking like that.

(*f*) I will surely drown. Will no one save me.

4. Parse the word *like* in (*b*).

It *little profits* that, an idle *King*.
By this still hearth, among these barren crags,
Matched with an aged wife, I mete and dole
Unequal laws unto a savage race,
That hoard, and sleep, and feed, and know not me.
Parse *little, profits, King, matched.*

5. But though I'll gladly trace these scenes with thee,
Yet the sweet converse of an innocent mind
Whose words are images of thoughts refined,
Is my soul's pleasure : and it sure must be
  Almost the highest bliss of human kind
When to thy haunts, two kindred spirits flee.

[Write out each subordinate or dependent clause by itself, and tell the kind (noun, adjective, adverb). Point out the word or words to which it relates, and state whether the sentence should be regarded as complex or compound.]

NOTE.—An analysis of subjects or predicates is not desired.

II.

1. (The following letter must not be less than fifteen, nor more than twenty lines in length. It will be marked in form, punctuation, construction and subject-matter. Please append an outlined

and properly addressed envelope, and write the letter on a sheet by itself.)

(*a*) Imagine it is mid-summer. Write a letter inviting a school-friend to visit you for two weeks. Tell her what your amusements are, by what railroad she must travel, when the trains leave, etc., and express your anxiety to see her.

(*b*) Envelope.

2. Give five verbs beginning with the following prefixes : (1) *a, ab.*—(2) *ad.*—(3) *e, ex.*—(4) *pre.*—(5) *re.* Use each verb in a separate simple sentence.

3. Define collation, collision, collusion, barometer, thermometer, and use two of these words in two compound sentences.

4. (*a*) What means the proverbial phrase : A bird in the hand is worth two in the bush.

(*b*) Give the proverbial phrase based on one of the characteristics of a precious metal, and expressing the idea that we ought not to be deceived by appearances, by the impression certain things make on the eye.

(*c*) Give the feminine forms of emperor, executor and hero, and use one of the masculine and one of the feminine forms, each, in a separate complex sentence.

(*d*) Form a noun from the adjective content, and use the noun contents in any sentence.

5. Capitalize and punctuate the following :

Every general of prominence had a nickname bestowed upon him by his troops some of these names were of a sarcastic nature but usually they indicated the confidence of the men in their leaders or their admiration for them gen. grant was commonly known over the watchfires of the army of the potomac as old united states from the initials of his name but sometimes he was called old three stars that number indicating his rank as lieutenant-general mcclellan was endeared to his army as little mac meade who wore spectacles was delighted to learn that his men had named him four-eyed george for he knew it was not intended as a reproach.

GEOGRAPHY.

1. (*a*) How many degrees is New York from Greenwich, England ?

(*b*) What is the distance in geographical miles between New York and the Equator ?

(*c*) At Valparaiso the time is 10 min. earlier than New York time.   What is its longitude ?

(*d*) What is the longitude of a place exactly half-way round the globe (east or west) from New York ?

(*e*) What is the latitude of a place on the Arctic circle ?

2. (*a*) Give as nearly as you can the direction of the following places from New York, (*a*) Salt Lake City, (*b*) Albany, N. Y., (*c*) Washington, D. C., (*d*) London, England, and (*e*) the Caspian Sea.

(*b*) In what direction do the Allegheny Mountains extend ?

(*c*) State as nearly as you can the general direction in which Columbus sailed in going from Spain to San Salvador.

(*d*) In what group of islands did he first discover land?

(*e*) Where is the river Orinoco ?   Where is the peninsula of Yucatan ?

3. Bound the State of Michigan and give its capital city.

4. (*a*) Name the States or Territories which form the northern border of the United States.

(*b*) In what States do the Mississippi and the Missouri rivers, respectively, rise ?

5. (*a*) Name the State which produces the largest amount of coal.

(*b*) Name two great grain producing States.

(*c*) From what portions of the United States are the greatest supplies of iron obtained ?

(*d*) In what parts are found the greatest supplies of precious metals ?

(*e*) What is the principal export of New Orleans ?

6. (*a*) Through what parts of the world do the following

mountains extend, (*a*) the Caucasus, (*b*) the Himalayas, (*c*) the Pyrenees.

(*b*) Name two active volcanoes, stating in what countries they are situated.

7. (*a*) Name the largest river of (*a*) Africa,(*b*) South America and (*c*) Europe, stating in what part each rises and where it terminates.

(*b*) Name four large rivers you would cross in going from New York to Columbus, Ohio.

8. (*a*) To what nations do the following islands belong, (*a*) Cuba, (*b*) Jamaica, (*c*) New Guinea, (*d*) Luzon ?

(*b*) Give as near as you can the location of the Hawaiian or Sandwich Islands.

9. What is the form of Government of Brazil ? of Russia ? of Switzerland ? of Great Britain ? of Canada ?

10. Name the countries bordering the Mediterranean Sea on the south, stating which are not independent and what nations govern them.

HISTORY.

1. (*a*) What proofs show that America was inhabited by a race of men previous to the Indians ?

(*b*) What name have we applied to these people

(*c*) Who was the first navigator who circumnavigated the earth ?

(*a*) Where and when was the first permanent settlement made by the Dutch ?

2. (*a*) Who were the English Puritans ?

(*b*) Why did they leave England ?

(*c*) Who was King of England in 1620 ?

(*d*) Who was the first Governor of the Puritans ?

(*e*) What name did the Dutch give their colony on Manhattan Island ? How was the island obtained ?

3. (*a*) In what year and by whom was New York taken from the Dutch ?

(*b*) Who had command of the British army at the commencement of the Revolution?

(*c*) Name three battles fought in 1775?

(*d*) Name the members of the Committee appointed by Congress to draft the Declaration of Independence.

(*e*) What was the most disastrous battle to the Americans in 1776?

4. (*a*) What two rebellions occurred between 1787 and 1794? State the cause of each.

(*b*) During whose administration were the Alien and Sedition Laws passed?

(*c*) Explain the Missouri Compromise.

(*d*) Explain briefly the Fugitive Slave Law.

5. (*a*) By what two great battles was Lee driven back when he tried to invade the North?

(*b*) When was the fight between the Merrimac and Monitor? Describe it.

(*c*) Who were the nominees for the Presidency in 1864?

(*d*) When and by whom was Abraham Lincoln assassinated?

(*e*) Who succeeded him as President?

SPELLING.

" After the battle of *Gettysburg*, Meade's *campaign* in *Virginia* had been *inconclusive*. The leading *members* of the *Committee* on the *Conduct* of the War urged that he should be *removed*. They were in favor of the *reappointment* of *Hooker*, but would *acquiesce* in that of any other general whom the President should think better fitted for the place. But all eyes had been turned to Grant, and it was *tacitly conceded* that he should be made the *commander* of all the armies in the field. For this purpose the grade of *lieutenant-general* was *revived*, and his *commission* was *formally presented* to him by the President. *Henceforth* the control of *military operations* was to be in the hands of a soldier free from the *dictation* of *civilian authority*, even that of Mr. Stanton, the *Secretary* of War."

Grant rode over a *rough* road to *Chattanooga* from *Nashville, Tennessee.*

Sherman's march from *Atlanta* to *Savannah* and thence to *Raleigh* is perhaps the most *brilliant recorded* in history.

Alabaster.	*Farinaceous.*	*Parasite.*
Brigantine.	*Galley.*	*Query.*
Carrot (a vegetable).	*Harangue.*	*Recommend.*
	Iterate.	*Sicily.*
Caret (wanting).	*Jocular.*	*Toledo.*
Carat (the weight for the fineness of gold).	*Knapsack.*	*Utah.*
	Litigation.	*Vesuvius* (mount).
	Manacle.	*Wilkesbarre.*
Delicacy.	*Nauseate.*	
Emissary.	*Ocular.*	

College of the City of New York, 1894.

ARITHMETIC.

1. (a) What is meant by ratio?
   (b) If 3 is subtracted from 8, and 5 obtained, what names are given to 3, 8, and 5 respectively?
   (c) What is a decimal fraction?
   (d) What is meant by the least common multiple (or least common dividend) of several numbers?

2. Find the values of the following:
   (a) $\frac{4}{7}$ of $3\frac{1}{2} \times \frac{2}{3}$.

   (b) $\frac{\frac{3}{4}}{\frac{1}{5}}$ of $1\frac{1}{3}$ of 3.

   (c) $\frac{3}{4} + \frac{\frac{1}{5}}{\frac{2}{3}} + \frac{1}{3}$ of $4\frac{1}{2}$.

3. (a) Multiply $\frac{2}{3}$ by $\frac{4}{5}$, and give the rule for multiplying one common fraction by another.
   (b) Explain the reason of this rule, using the above example as an illustration.

4. (a) Write in decimal form: Three, and ten one-thousandths; three hundred, and three one-thousandths; ten, and twenty-five ten-thousandths.
   (b) Reduce $\frac{7}{8}$ to a decimal fraction.
   (c) Multiply .0015 by 3.2.
   (d) Divide 16.4 by .041.

5. (a) Reduce 3 oz. to the decimal of a ton.
   (b) If in a decimal fraction the decimal point be moved one place to the right, what effect will this produce on the value of the fraction?
   (c) Explain the reason of this.

6. (a) What part of 5 is 2?
   (b) What part of $\frac{4}{5}$ is $\frac{3}{8}$?
   (c) What per cent. of $\frac{4}{5}$ is $\frac{3}{8}$?

7. Four men were engaged to build a wall in 10 days. At the end of 5 days they found that only ¼ of the wall was built. How many additional men would be needed to complete the wall in the given time ?

8. A can do a piece of work in 24 days; A and C can do it in 8 days; B and C can do it in 7¼ days. In what time can B alone do it ?

9. A man bought a farm for $20,000 cash, and sold it again immediately, taking in payment $2,010 in cash, and a note at six months without interest for the remainder. He had this note discounted at the bank, and then found that the total amount of cash he had received was seven per cent. more than the cost of the farm. What was the face of the note ?

10. A real estate dealer bought a country cottage and lot for $2,000, and rented it at once for $300 for the summer. He insured the house for $1,400, paying one per cent. premium. The house was burned before the end of the season, and the tenant paid him only $200 rent; but the insurance was paid in full, and he sold the ground for $500. Did he make or lose on the transaction, and how much ?

ENGLISH.

N.B.—In analyzing, you will state the kind of each sentence analyzed, whether simple, compound, or complex. You will write each clause separately, stating whether it is co-ordinate or subordinate, etc., and indicating to what word each clause relates. Give the principal parts of each clause. Point out to what the modifying words and phrases relate. If you can, do all this in the form of diagram.

Write your letter, which is not to contain more than nine sentences, on a separate sheet of paper. Address it to Robert Wilson, and sign Edward Jackson. Be careful to give date, address, and signature correctly. Other points to be attended to are spelling, capitalization, punctuation, grammatical correctness, the sense and clearness of your sentences, their orderly arrangement, and the composition generally. Let the letter be neatly written.

I. Analyze :

(1) To err is human, to forgive, divine. (Pope.)

(2) From a child I was fond of reading, and all the little

money that came into my hands, was ever laid out in
books.   (Franklin.)

(3) Ill fares the land, to hastening ills a prey,
Where wealth accumulates and men decay ;
For a bold peasantry, their country's pride,
When once destroyed, can never be supplied.

(Goldsmith.)

II. Write a letter on either of the following subjects :

(1) A visit to the menagerie in Central Park.

(2) A day's experience in school.

GEOGRAPHY.

1. How much of the surface of the earth is land? What
portions of the land are not habitable? Why? Of what
regions is it not known whether they are land or water?

2. Which rivers join their waters at Kansas City? Which
near St. Louis? Which at Cairo (Ill.)? Which at Pittsburg?
Which near Troy (N. Y.)? Which at Montreal? Which near
Buenos Ayres? Which at Lyons? Which at Mayence?
Which at Belgrade? Which near Bassorat (Asiatic Turkey)?

3. Name the countries about the North Sea ; those about
the Baltic ; those about the Adriatic ; those about the Black
Sea ; those about the Japan Sea.

4. Name the four largest islands in the West Indies ; the
four largest in Malaysia ; the most important city in the first
group, and the most important city in the second ; tell of each
city on which island it is situated, and what is its general or
official language.

5. Name five great mountain ranges, two in North America,
one in South America, one in Europe, and one in Asia ; tell
of each, as nearly as you can, in which part of the Grand
Division it is. Name the highest peak in the Eastern Hemi-
sphere, and the highest in the Western, and state how high
each is. Name three volcanoes, and locate them.

6. Between the mouth of the Pigeon River (which river
flows into Lake Superior on the confines of Minnesota and Ontario) and the Thousand Islands, the United States and the

Dominion of Canada approach very near to each other four times ; name the rivers which separate them, and locate them with reference to the Lakes and the American States. Where is the Strait of Dover? Where the Strait of Gibraltar? Where the Strait of Bal-el-Mandeb? Where the Strait of Magellan ?

7. Locate the following capes—Clear, Cod, Comorin, East, Farewell, Finisterre, Good Hope, Hatteras, Land's End, Lopatka, May, Race, St. Roque, San Lucas, Verde.

8. What is the Magnetic Pole? Where is it? What is a meridian? Omaha and Vera Cruz lie on the same meridian, and Vera Cruz is about twenty-two degrees south of Omaha ; what time is it at Vera Cruz, when it is noon at Omaha? Does the sun ever rise at the same time in these two cities? Does it generally rise in one city earlier than in the other?

HISTORY.

1. Give an account of the explorations and discoveries of Vespucius, Verazzani, Champlain, and Hudson.

2. In what way were Raleigh, Roger Williams, the Duke of York, and General Oglethorpe identified with the settlement of this country ?

Give particulars in each case.

3. Give the history of the Stamp Act and the Boston Port Bill.

4. The battles of Bunker Hill and Camden.—Show how they came to be fought, and add a brief description of each.

5. What were the boundaries of the United States, as fixed by treaty at the close of the Revolutionary War? How were they changed in 1803 ?

6. State the causes of the Mexican War. What advantage did the United States gain by it?

7. Name the Presidents who served two terms ; also those who died in office.

8. What services did General Grant render this country during the Civil War?

9. Ericsson, Samuel Adams, Perry, Hamilton, Nathan Hale. —Why are these names prominent in our history?

10. What are the principal features of the government of the State of New York? Who was its first Governor?

Normal College.

ARITHMETIC.

1. Give the sum in units of lower denominations of .67 league, $\frac{5}{8}$ mile and $\frac{9}{10}$ rod.

2. $\frac{.035+.00128}{.07+.016} \times \frac{.0374 \times .0075}{.675-.6357}$. Simplify and express the result as a common fraction reduced to its lowest terms.

3. A builder sold a house to an agent at a profit of 20%. The agent sold to a third party at a gain of 15%, who in turn sold it at a loss of 8% and lost $2,000. Find the cost of the house and for what it was sold each time.

4. A house cost $15,725 and rents for $1,500; the insurance is $\frac{1}{4}$% and the repairs $\frac{6}{10}$% each year. What rate of interest does it pay?

5. A broker buys stock when it is 20% below par and sells it when it is 16% below par. What is the rate of gain?

6. Gunpowder is composed of 33 parts by weight, of saltpetre, 7 of charcoal, and 5 of sulphur. Find the percentage composition of gunpowder.

7. A ship sailed due south and due east on alternate days at the same rate each day; at the end of six days it was found to be 203.646 miles southeast from the place of starting. What was the daily rate of sailing?

8. An orchard containing 6 acres 12 sq. rods, is three times as long as it is wide. Required the length and breadth.

9. A man who owned $20,000 of stock, par value, sold for 140 and invested the proceeds in other stock at 160. The first stock paid an annual dividend of 5% and the second of $6\frac{1}{2}$%. What was the change in his income?

10. Required the number of square feet in one face of a cubical block whose contents are 405,244 cubic feet.

DRAWING.

1. Draw a regular pentagon, four inches on a side.

2. Draw a regular octagon, four inches on a side.

3. Draw any Greek or Moresque ornament, writing name underneath.

4. Draw from the solid in position—actual size.

Working lines must be left on the paper. Ruling is not
. allowed.

ENGLISH.

1. From the word *syllable* form five other words and define each word.

2. Define the following words : *fare, pun, fain, caret* and *idiom.*

3. Write a composition on *Benjamin Franklin,* stating (1) where·born, (2) father's trade, (3) his own trade, (4) where he worked at his trade when he arrived at manhood, (5) what public offices he held and his influence in securing American independence.*

4. Write fifteen lines of poetry which you committed to memory (in accordance with the new course of study).

   (*a*) Define *poetry, verse, stanza.*

   (*b*) What is the difference between *rhyme* and *rhythm?*

5. Punctuate and capitalize the following : .

   The Moors brought into Spain the cultivation of the Sugar Cane of Cotton and Rice and the Mulberry on which feeds the Silkworm commerce owed them the blades of toledo the Silks of grenada, the leather of cordova the Spices and sweets of Valencia were renowned throughout Europe at this period the moors had accustomed themselves to forget the Past and to seek no other successes than those of Industry.

6. What is the meaning of the proverbial phrase : "Birds

---

* *Credit will be given for correct sentences, the right use of words, correct punctuation, the right use of capitals, and for brevity and clearness of expression. You must write at least twenty-five lines.*

of a feather flock together?" Give any other common proverb and explain it.

Give for each of the following a word of Saxon origin having the same meaning: *Advent, omnipotent, precursor, prospect, ultimate.*

Give the plural of *leaf, son-in-law, sheep, pailful, stratum.*

ENGLISH GRAMMAR.

"Cousin, I am too young to be your father,
  Though you are old enough to be my heir.
  What you will have, I'll give, and willing too ;
  For do we must what force will have us do."

1. Analyze the two sentences :
  (a) To what kind of sentence does each belong?
  (b) Write out the clause or clauses and tell the kind (noun, adjective, adverbial).

2. Parse *cousin, father, enough, what* (in the third line), *do* (at the end of fourth line) and *willing.*

3. Correct the following sentences and give the reasons :
  (a) " It is our duty to protect this government and that flag from every assailant, be they whom they may."
  (b) "I can give no information concerning *who* or *whom* * were there."
  (c) "His curiosity as well as his anxiety *were* or *was* * excited."
  Which forms are correct, and why?

4. Define *part of speech, case, voice, syntax.* Tell why the same word may belong to different parts of speech.

5. With any abstract noun construct a simple sentence, and then expand it into a complex sentence, making the dependent clause adverbial.

Classify as nouns, adjectives, or adverbials the italicized clauses :

I know the hour *when he arrived.*

'I know *when he left the city.*

I was not at home *when he called.*

* Which pronoun? Which verb?

GEOGRAPHY.

1 (*a*) How can you tell in the day-time, without a mariner's compass, where the true south is?

    (*b*) In what parts of the world is the sun directly overhead, at noon, twice in the year?

    (*c*) When it is 11 A.M. at 100° W., what is the true time in New York?

    (*d*) What is the latitude of *Madrid?*

2. Name ten States through which you would pass if you travelled directly west from New York City, and the capital of each.

3. Bound *Idaho ;* name its capital city. Where is the *Yellowstone Park ?*

4. Locate the following cities : *Omaha, Galveston, Cleveland, Louisville, Little Rock, Christiania, Lhassa, Berne, Herat, Bombay.*

5. (*a*) Why is the climate of *Newfoundland* more severe than that of *Ireland?*

    (*b*) Which of these islands lies farther north?

    (*c*) What river runs between the U. S. and Mexico?

    (*d*) Describe the geographical position of *Nicaragua.*

6. State where the following rivers rise ; where they empty. Name a large city on each and the nation to which that city belongs. (*a*) the Ohio ; (*b*) the St. Lawrence ; (*c*) the Danube ; (*d*) the Rhone ; (*e*) the Paraguay.

7. (*a*) What group of islands on the eastern coast of Asia are in the same latitude as our middle Atlantic States?

    (*b*) What large island lies south of Australia?

    (*c*) What one south of Hindostan?

    (*d*) To what islands was Napoleon Bonaparte exiled?

8. (*a*) What mountains would you cross in going from Bordeaux to Barcelona? (*b*) From Vienna to Venice? (*c*) From Bulgaria to Constantinople? (*d*) From Tennessee into North Carolina? (*e*) Name two volcanoes in Europe, one in Mexico, and two in South America.

9. (*a*) In what two river valleys were the most ancient civilizations of the world situated?

(b) Where are the " Pillars of Hercules "?

(c) Name three countries in which Mohammedanism is the prevailing religion, and

(d) two in which the Greek Church prevails.

10. (a) Name the two principal railroads between New York and Buffalo.

(b) What are the following great routes between the East and the Pacific respectively called?

1. That which passes through Bismarck and Helena?

2. That which passes through Salt Lake City?

3. That which passes through Winnipeg?

HISTORY.

I.

1. The invention of what instrument assisted naval exploration?

2. Who was King of Mexico, when Cortez came to that country?

3. Who made the first and who the second voyage around the world?

4. What were the French and Indian wars and their dates?

5. When and where were negro slaves first sold in America?

6. What was the most important event in the last French and Indian war and its date?

7. What reason did the English Government give for taxing the American colonies? How did Great Britain interfere with American commerce?

II.

1. Where and when did the first Continental Congress assemble?

2. Who was chiefly instrumental in writing the Declaration of Independence?

3. What city did Washington take at the beginning of 1776, and what city at the end of the same year?

4. What important battle of the Revolutionary War in-

duced France to enter into an alliance with the Americans ?
Its date and the commanders on both sides ? What event was
decisive of the war ?   Its date and the commanders on both
sides ?

5. Name one noted Frenchman, German, and Polander, who
assisted the American revolutionary cause.

6. Where and when did the first Federal Congress meet
after the adoption of the Constitution ?

7. When was the City of Washington made the capital of
the United States ?

8. From whom and for what amount was Louisiana purchased ?

III.

1. Under whose administration did the war of 1812 begin
and end ?

2. What Indian troubles occurred during the administration
of Jackson ?

3. Why was the petition of Texas for admission to the
Union at first rejected ?

    When was she admitted ?

4. Whose administrations extended from March 4th, 1849,
to March 4th, 1853 ?

5. When was gold discovered in California ?

IV.

1. What State passed the first ordinance of secession and
when ?

2. What vessels were sunk by the Merrimac?

3. By what vessel was the Merrimac disabled ?

4. Name five great victories won by General Grant, three by
General Lee, and one by General Sheridan.

5. What were the charges against Johnson, and what was
the result of his impeachment?

6. When, of whom, and for what consideration was Alaska
obtained?

V.

1. What was the debt of the Union, August 31st, 1865?

2. When did Congress demonetize silver? When and by what bill was it again made legal tender? When was this bill repealed?

3. How was the Chinese immigration restricted in 1882?

4. Who was the first American writer to secure general recognition at home and abroad?

5. What are the three branches of the Federal Government? Who presides over the Senate? What is the presiding officer of the House of Representatives called?

Spelling.

At the time when he became King of Spain, Cabot, Columbus, and Vespucius had discovered the continent of America. Not long after his accession to the crown, Fernando Cortez, with a handful of men, marched from the Gulf of Mexico upon the city of the same name, and, after terrible struggles, dethroned its sovereign and reigned in his stead as Charles' viceroy. He discovered the Pacific and California. Before Charles' death, the Spaniards pushed northwards to New Mexico, and southwards to the Isthmus of Panama.

Trisyllable	Surfeited
Tierce	Maintenance
Bevy	Misdemeanor
Jocular	Oracle
Bizarre	Palate
Caviler	Saracen
Belligerent	Doggerel
Vestige	Syringe
Elegy	Labyrinth
Synonym	Oxygen
Privilege	Tenable
Filigree	Solecism
Hyperbole	Corinth
Irritated	Vesuvius
Thibet	Bosphorus

College of the City of New York, 1895.

ARITHMETIC.

1. (a) What is a decimal fraction ?   Give an example.

   (b) What is a denominate number ?   Give an example.

   (c) Give the rule for multiplying one common fraction by another.

   (d) Define ratio.

2. (a) Reduce to a simple fraction

$$\tfrac{3}{4} \text{ of } 4\tfrac{1}{2} \times \frac{\frac{2}{3}}{\frac{4}{5}} \text{ of } \tfrac{3}{5}.$$

   (b) Add $\tfrac{3}{8}$, $\tfrac{2}{3}$, and $\tfrac{5}{12}$.

   (c) What part of $\tfrac{5}{8}$ is $\tfrac{2}{3}$?

3. (a) Find the value of $\tfrac{3}{61}$ of a mile in whole numbers of lower denominations.

   (b) Reduce .00125 to a common fraction in its lowest terms.

   (c) What is the difference between .325 and $\tfrac{5}{8}$?

4. (a) What effect is produced upon the value of a common fraction by multiplying numerator and dominator by the same quantity ?

   (b) Explain why this is so.

5. (a) Subtract .003 from 1.1.

   (b) Multiply 1.04 by 100.1.

   (c) Divide 1.111 by .0011.

   (d) What effect is produced upon a decimal by moving the decimal point one place to the right ?

   (e) Explain why this is so.

6. I bought 100 shares of Railroad Stock at 10% below par, and sold them at 8% above par.   What amount of money did I make, and what percentage did I gain on my investment ?

7. A cistern has three pipes. The first can fill it in four hours, the second in five hours, and the third in six hours. After the first had been running alone for two hours it was closed, and the second opened and allowed to run for two hours, and

then closed, and the third opened. How long did the third have to run in order to fill the cistern?

8. Two brothers each received at the same time $980 in cash. The first bought R. R. Stock at 2% discount, and sold the same at the end of a year at 2% premium. The other placed his money in a Savings Bank, which paid 2% compound interest every six months. How much did each have at the end of the year?

9. A contractor undertook to build a wall in twenty days, and set six men at work on it. At the end of eight days he found they had only been able to build ⅓ of it. How many *more* men did he have to put on the job, in order to complete the wall in the time agreed upon?

10. A and B set out from two cities 720 miles apart, and travel toward each other. A goes 12 miles more each day than B, and at the end of ten days they meet. What has been the rate of travel per day of each?

ENGLISH.

I. Analyze the following extract, classifying the sentence, describing each clause, and giving the principal parts with their word and phrase adjuncts.

"Nevertheless, the common sense of mankind, which in questions of this sort seldom goes far wrong, will always recognize a distinction between crimes which originate in an inordinate zeal for the commonwealth, and crimes which originate in selfish cupidity."—MACAULAY.

II. Explain the difference between an active transitive verb and a passive verb. State how a passive verb is formed. Using the verb "*strike*," construct two sentences, one with the verb in the active voice, the other with the verb in the passive voice. Underline the passive verb.

III. 1. Write not more than ten lines from some poem you have memorized during the past school year, giving the name of the poem and its author. In writing this extract, pay particular attention to the poetical arrangement by lines, the spelling, the punctuation, and the use of capitals.

2. Tell in your own language what the author means in the selection you have given.

IV. Rewrite the following sentences correctly, stating briefly the grammatical reasons for each correction:

1. Of the pair of horses, the shortest one seemed to be much the younger.

2. We did not tell her who the package came from.

3. Nearly every one of the students we knew were going to the exhibition.

4. An old shoe always goes on very easy.

5. She was smaller than either of her three sisters.

V. 1. "Then a book was still a book,
      Where a wistful man might look,
      Finding *something* through the whole
      Beating—like a human *soul*."

Parse the words in italics.

2. Change the following extract into a simple sentence:

"This assault which was of a cruel and barbarous nature, was committed by soldiers who belonged to the British army."

VI. Write, on a separate sheet, a composition on one of the following subjects:

1. The Greater New York.

2. Military Drill in the Schools.

3. A letter to your uncle in the country, describing some object or place of interest of New York City.

NOTE.—Your composition, or letter, must not be less than one hundred or more than one hundred and fifty words. In your letter, address your uncle as Jonathan Swift, and sign it Alexander Pope.

GEOGRAPHY.

1. What is the shape of the earth? Give reasons for your statement.

2. Name and define the circles of the earth; the zones; the divisions of land; of water.

3. Where are the following islands situated: Anticosti, Yezo, Man, Sicily, Aleutian, Samoan, Azores, Jamaica, Bermuda, Iceland?

4. Name the sources of the following rivers, and state their general course, and the waters into which they empty : Yangtse-kiang, Murray, Yukon, Columbia, Parana, Danube, Obi, Ohio, Ottawa, and St. Lawrence.

5. What countries border on the Mediterranean Sea; the Caribbean Sea; the China Sea; the Japan Sea; Bering's Sea?

6. In or between what countries or States are the following mountains: Pyrenees, Himalaya, Darling, Wahsatch, Atlas? The following bodies of water : Caspian Sea, Lake Superior, Victoria Nyanza, Lake Maracaybo, Cayuga Lake?

7. What States border on the Atlantic Ocean ; the Pacific Ocean ; the Dominion of Canada?

8. Name and locate five harbors on our Eastern, three on our Western, and two on our Southern coast.

9. Name the mountains, rivers, and lakes, great railroads, products, capital, and chief city of New York State.

10. What is meant by a solar day; by new or standard time; by an astronomical day? What is the latitude and longitude of New York City? Upon what does the difference in time of two places depend?

HISTORY.

1. The Constitution of the United States.—State when, where, and why it was adopted.

2. Name the Presidents in order, with dates of terms, from Madison's to Grant's administration inclusive.

3. What large tracts of territory has this country acquired through purchase? What through war? And what through annexation?

4. What events occurred within the present limits of New York and Brooklyn during the Revolutionary War?

5. Describe the early colonists of Virginia, Pennsylvania, and Rhode Island, showing in what respects they differed from each other.

6. What navigators discovered our Atlantic Coast from the St. Lawrence to Florida? Give their nationality and the part of the coast explored by each.

Of the four remaining questions answer any two.

7. Describe General Lee's invasion of the north, and his repulse, in 1863. What important events in the same year along the line of the Mississippi?

8. The State of New York.—Describe the form and general features of its government. How were we governed here in colonial times, both Dutch and English?

9. Give a clear account of the origin of the Revolution (about half a page).

10. What public services were rendered to the country by Thomas Jefferson, Daniel Webster, Nathaniel Greene, Wm. H. Seward, Wm. T. Sherman?

Normal College.

ARITHMETIC.

1. What mixed number multiplied by $\frac{1\frac{1}{2}}{\frac{2}{3}}$ equals $15\frac{3}{8}$?

2. A can do a piece of work in $\frac{3}{4}$ of a day, B can do it in $\frac{4}{5}$ of a day, and C can do it in $1\frac{1}{3}$ days. In what time can all do it, working together?

3. Divide 3 hundredths by 987 millionths.

4. $26\frac{1}{2}$ bushels of wheat are raised from $\frac{1}{2}$ bushel. What per cent is the increase?

5. A house that rents for $1,200 costs $16,000; the insurance is $\frac{4}{5}$ per cent., and the repairs $\frac{6}{10}$ per cent. What rate of interest does it pay?

6. If $2,000 in 6 mo. 15 da. produce $102.33, what principal must be loaned to gain $62.16 in 11 mo. 21 da.?

7. A's capital was in trade 6 mo., B's 8 mo., and C's 10 mo. A's gain was $750, B's $1,200, and C's $800, and the whole capital $19,880. How much did each own?

8. In what time will $18.20 at $5\frac{3}{4}$ per cent. amount to $28.43?

9. The diameter of a circle is 14 inches. What is the side of an inscribed square? (Inscribe the square.)

10. What is the difference between the true and the bank discount of $10,000 for 7½ mo. at 3½ per cent., no allowance being made for three days of grace?

DRAWING.

1. Draw an ellipse, vertical diameter 8 inches, horizontal diameter 5 inches.

2. Draw an octagon, 4 inches on a side.

3. Draw any Greek or Moresque ornament, writing name underneath.

4. Draw from the solid in position, actual size.

Working lines must be left on the paper. Ruling is not allowed.

ENGLISH.

1 (a) Define the following words : Analysis, synthesis, concrete, abstract, involution.

   (b) Write the plural of the first two words.

   (c) Write a compound sentence, using the words analysis and synthesis.

   (d) Write a sentence in which concrete is used as an adjective, and another in which the adjective may be used as a noun.

   (e) By substitution of another prefix change into words of opposite meaning : Inculpate, subscription, prologue.

40%

2. (a) Write five words derived from the word fame ; three from prime and two from idol.

   (b) What are synonyms? Give a synonym of torrid. Give a word in which one of the constituent parts of synonym is found and illustrate by an example. (The word synthesis will not be accepted.)   40%

3. (a) Draw a form of rectangular envelope and address it to a board of school trustees in some ward.

   (b) Write a letter of application to this board for a position as a teacher.   30%

4. Write a composition of not less than twenty or more than thirty lines on the City of New York, stating in order (1) its

boundaries ; (2) its early settlement ; (3) its subsequent con-
quest ; (4) why it was named New York ; (5) to what it owes
its greatness as a city ; and (6) name its principal buildings
and parks.   60%

(In 3 and 4 credit will be given for arrangement, correct use
of words, punctuation and grammatical construction.)

5. Capitalize and punctuate :

The aziola.

Do you hear the aziola cry
methinks she must be nigh
said mary as we sate
in dusk ere the stars were lit or candles brought
and i who thought
this aziola was some tedious woman
asked who is aziola how elate
i felt to know that it was nothing human
no mockery of myself to fear or hate
and mary saw my soul
and laughed and said disquiet yourself not
'tis nothing but a little downy owl.   30%

(Students are requested, in writing their answers and num-
bering their papers, to follow the order of the questions.)

GRAMMAR.

1. Name five adjectives that do not admit of comparison.
Name the two positives of *worse.*   Write the plural of *radius,*
of *bandit* and of *stratum.*

2.   ` *This was the noblest Roman of them all :*
All the conspirators, save only he
Did that they did in envy of great Cæsar ;
He only, in a general honest thought
And common good to all, made one of them.

(*a*) Analyze the above sentence, stating the kind of
sentence.

(*b*) Write the several clauses.

(*c*) Correct errors (if any).

3. Parse *save, that, only* (in second line), *only* (in fourth line), *good.*

4. Compose a sentence having a substantive clause used as an attribute.

   Write a sentence containing an adverbial clause, and change the clause into a phrase.

   Write a simple sentence having its object modified by a participial phrase, and change the phrase into an adjective clause.

5. Correct the following sentences and give the reasons :

   (*a*) Either you or I are in the way.

   (*b*) That is seldom or ever the case.

   (*c*) What sounds have each of the vowels ?

   (*d*) Bismarck is greater than any German statesman.

GEOGRAPHY.

1. Name the boundaries and state the width of the Torrid and Temperate zones.

   (*a*) At what place on the globe must one be to have the sun in the zenith on the 21st of June ?

   (*b*) Of what use are parallels and meridians ?

   (*c*) State the latitude and longitude of New York.

   (*d*) Why does a telegram from New York at noon reach Omaha before noon ?

2. Name the straits and rivers which connect the great lakes with each other and with the ocean.

   (*a*) What is the population of the United States, of New York City, and of London ?   (In round numbers.)

   (*b*) Name two important islands belonging to the State of New York, and the largest town in each.

3. Draw a map of Connecticut, and locate the following cities : New Haven, Hartford, and Bridgeport.

   (*a*) Write the boundaries of the State.

4. Locate the following cities : Denver, Rock Island, Davenport, Vicksburg, Helena, Louisville, Olympia, Santa Fé, Bangor, and Chattanooga.

5. Name five rivers of South America.

(*a*) Bound Austria. State its capital and principal river.
(*b*) Name the two principal cities of Japan.
(*c*) What circle crosses the island of Formosa ?
(*d*) Name the Barbary States and the capital of each.
(*e*) Name two of the Sandwich Islands.
(*f*) On which is Honolulu situated ?

UNITED STATES HISTORY.

1. (*a*) To what race are the North American Indians supposed to belong? (*b*) What was the social condition of the Mexicans when attacked by Cortez? (*c*) Who discovered the Mississippi, and in what year ?

2. (*a*) When and by whom was slavery introduced into the United States ? (*b*) Describe briefly the difference in character between the original settlers of Massachusetts and Virginia. (*c*) Name the wars that preceded the French and Indian War.

3. (*a*) What name was given to the adherents of George III. during the war of the Revolution ? (*b*) What special experience as military officers had Washington and some of the other American commanders when the war was begun? (*c*) In what year did the Americans receive important aid from Europe, and from what nation? (*d*) Name the two most important battles of the Revolution, and give the date of each. (*e*) Name the battles in which Greene was chief commander.

4. (*a*) Give a brief account of the Hartford Convention. (*b*) What is meant by the Monroe Doctrine? (*c*) Name two noted American and two noted Mexican commanders during the Mexican War.

5. (*a*) Name the different commanders of the Army of the Potomac during the Civil War. (*b*) Name the two men who were Secretary of War under Lincoln. (*c*) What two great questions were settled by the success of the North? (*d*) Name the Presidents from Jackson to the present time.

SPELLING.

The military results of the campaign as summed up by Grant were : The defeat of the enemy in five battles outside of Vicksburg, the occupation of Jackson the capital of Mississippi, and the capture of Vicksburg, its garrison and munitions of war. He might have added the fall of Port Hudson which Farragut and Banks had vainly endeavored to reduce. ——Grant, after winning the battle of Chattanooga, sent Sherman to relieve Burnside who was cooped up in Knoxville, East Tennessee.——All eyes were turned to Grant, and it was tacitly conceded that he should command all the armies in the field. Two courses were open to him. He might invest Richmond from the north, or, crossing the Chickahominy and the James, besiege it from the south.

Anaconda	Vermilion	Embarrass
Bivouac	Vaccination	Javelin
Cannibal	Tureen	Murrain
Centennial	Symmetry	Morrisania
Centenary	Satyr	Philippine Islands
Cylinder	Resuscitate	Gibraltar
Declamatory	Rhythm	Jamaica
Inflammatory	Pomegranate	Tyrol
Diocese	Parricide	Sicily (Island)
Farinaceous	Palisade	Madeira
Graminivorous	Hyacinth	Mozambique
Victuals	Harass	Aleutian Islands

College of the City of New York, 1896.

ARITHMETIC.

1. (*a*) What is meant by the ratio of one number to another?
Give an example.

   (*b*) What is meant by the Greatest Common Divisor of
   three numbers? Give an example.

(c) What is meant by a compound fraction? Give an example?

(d) Give the rule for dividing one common fraction by another.

2. (a) Find the value of the following expressions:

$$\frac{\frac{1}{2} \text{ of } \frac{4}{5}}{\frac{3}{4} \text{ of } 1\frac{1}{3}} \div \frac{1}{8} \text{ of } \frac{3}{4} \text{ of } \frac{14}{7}.$$

(b) Add—

$$\frac{1}{2} + \frac{3}{5} + \frac{5}{16} + \frac{2}{7}.$$

(c) What part of $\frac{1}{2}$ is $\frac{1}{4}$?

3. A telephone wire whose length is 1 mile 30 rods, cost $10.50. What was the price of the wire per foot?

4. (a) Write in decimal form:

Three ten-thousandths,

Three, and ten one-thousandths,

One thousand and ten, and ten hundredths.

(b) What is the quotient of 2.25 by 1.5? by 150? by .009?

(c) Add 3.002, 610, 21.6.

5. (a) Divide $\frac{3}{4}$ by 7.

(b) If the denominator of a fraction is multiplied by a whole number, what effect will this produce upon the value of the fraction?

(c) Explain the reason of this.

6. (a) When a decimal fraction is multiplied by another decimal fraction, give the rule for pointing off the decimal places in the product.

(b) Explain the reason of this rule.

7. A man bought 1,000 bushels of potatoes at a certain price per bushel. One hundred bushels were damaged before he could sell them, but he sold the remainder for $55, and found he had gained 10 % on the cost of his entire purchase. What did he pay per bushel?

8. A dealer in real estate had his note for $20,000 at six months discounted at his bank, and with the proceeds bought a house. He rented this at $50 a month, for six months, but

during that time he paid out $240 for repairs. At the end of the six months he sold the property at an advance of 5 % on the original cost, and from the money he received paid his note at the bank. How much did he gain on the transaction?

9. Six men undertook to do a piece of work and finished half of it in 5 days. Then two of the men were taken off and set on another job. In how long a time did the remaining men finish the work?

10. A, B, and C entered into a partnership for three years. A put in $10,000, B $15,000, and C $25,000. At the end of the first year, however, A put in $10,000 more, B put in $2,500 more, C withdrew $12,500, and D joined the partnership and put in $25,000. At the end of the three years the profits were found to be $34,000. How much should each partner receive?

ENGLISH.

I.　　The snow had begun in the gloaming,
　　　　And busily all the night
　　　Had been heaping field and highway
　　　　With a silence deep and white.

　　　Every pine and fir and hemlock
　　　　Wore ermine too dear for an earl,
　　　And the poorest twig on the elm-tree
　　　　Was ridged inch deep with pearl.—*Lowell.*

In the above extract state what is meant by
　(a) " *In the gloaming.*"
　(b) " *With a silence deep and white.*"
　(c) " *Wore ermine too dear for an earl.*"
　(d) " *Was ridged inch deep with pearl.*"

II. 1. In the above extract analyze the first stanza, classifying the sentence, describing each clause, and giving the principal parts with their word and phrase adjuncts.

　2. Parse:
　(a) *had been heaping,* (b) *wore,* (c) *dear,* (d) *was ridged.*

III. Rewrite the following sentences correctly, stating briefly the grammatical reasons for each correction :

    1. The work goes on slower than we expected.

    2. His four sons were named John, Peter, Henry, and Robert ; the latter was a graduate of Harvard.

    3. Try to write like I do.

    4. Each of the boys were perfect in their spelling.

    5. Neither the carriage nor the livery of the servant who preceded it were familiar to them.

IV. On a separate sheet of paper write a letter, properly arranged, containing not less than one hundred or more than one hundred and fifty words. Imagine you were living near Lexington on April 19, 1775, and saw all you have studied, or that has been told you, about the story of the battle of Lexington. Write the letter to your cousin living in Philadelphia, and give an account of what you saw and heard on that memorable day. Sign your letter Jonathan Swift.

GEOGRAPHY.

    1. Name the grand divisions of land on the Earth, first in the order of size, and secondly in the order of population.

    2. Which is farther, from the Mississippi (at St. Louis) east to the Atlantic, or west to the Pacific ? Which is the longest distance and which the shortest of these three—from Cadiz (Spain) to Norfolk (Virginia), from San Francisco to Yokohama, from Sidney (New South Wales) to Valparaiso (Chile)?

    3. Name the two largest states of the United States; the two smallest ; the three east of the Mississippi that have neither seashore nor lakeshore ; the three on Lake Superior.

    4. Bound the State of New York (exclusive of Long Island), starting at Buffalo and following the boundary until you get back to Buffalo again ; and so far as lakes and rivers constitute the border, name not only them but also the land on the other side.

    5. Sketch the coast of South America from the Isthmus of Panama to the mouth of the Amazon ; start the boundary lines running from the coast inward ; name, on your sketch,

the republics and colonies so divided; locate the mouth of the Orinoco, and trace the general course of the river; locate and name the capitals which are on the coast.

6. Which two European countries have possessions in North America considerably larger than themselves? which four European countries have large possessions in Africa, other than Egypt? to which country is Egypt tributary? Where are the Hebrides? where the New Hebrides? where the Canary Islands? (name not only the ocean but also the nearest land).

7. Name ten European cities, not capitals, nor more than two in any one country; and name with each the country in which and the water on which it is situated.

8. Through which (four) straits must a ship pass on the way from Odessa (which is on the Black Sea) to Cronstadt (which is on the Gulf of Finland)? Which powers [or nations] have forts on these straits? Odessa being almost due south of Cronstadt, the latter on the 60th parallel and the former in latitude 46° 30', what is the distance, in English miles, between them? Could a ship-canal connecting the two ports be carried along their meridian, or are there mountains in the way?

HISTORY EXAMINATION.

1. Describe Raleigh's attempts to establish colonies in America. What did Gosnold accomplish?

2. Write a brief account of the settlement of Massachusetts, New York, and New Jersey.

3. Give an outline of the Parliamentary measures that provoked the colonists from 1765 to 1775.

4. What were the causes and the result of the 1812 war? Name three naval actions, 1813–14.

5. State the "Secession" question, giving the views of both parties. What was the "nullification" issue before that?

6. With what events are the following places associated in our history? Philadelphia, in 1774; Tippecanoe; Salem; Cowpens; Vicksburg; Detroit; Monterey.

Answer any *one*, and only one, of the following questions :

7. Name the Presidents in order, from Jackson to Garfield. Who was President when Alaska was purchased? Who, when gold was discovered in California? Who, when Hamilton was killed?

8. What are the leading points in the last three amendments to the Constitution?

9. Give an account of the earliest explorations of the Great Lakes and the Ohio and Mississippi valleys.

N. B.—The candidates will also be marked for their SPELLING on this paper. They should examine their work carefully before handing it in.

Normal College.

ARITHMETIC.

1. A certain sum of money was divided among four persons. A received $\frac{1}{4}$, B $\frac{1}{4}$, C $\frac{3}{14}$, and D the remainder, which is $30. What was the whole sum divided?

2. Divide one thousand and one hundred thousandths by one thousandth.

3. Invested $6,000 in 6 per cent. bonds at 125. What rate per cent. do I receive, and what is the income from it?

4. Find the cost of covering the floor of a hall, 45 feet long and 6 feet 6 inches wide, with oil-cloth at $1.35 a square yard.

5. What principal will amount to $15,000 in $4\frac{1}{2}$ years at $5\frac{1}{2}$ per cent.?

6. Bought goods for $500; sold half of them at a loss of 20 per cent., and the other half at a gain of 20 per cent. How much shall I gain or lose on the whole?

7. A and B are partners; $\frac{1}{4}$ of A's capital is equal to $\frac{1}{3}$ of B's; and their loss in business is $2,150. What is the share of each?

8. A rectangular field is 42 rods long and 35 rods wide. Find its value at $37.50 an acre.

9. What is the length of the diagonal of a city lot, 25 feet by 100 feet?

10. Find the cube root of 3 to three decimal places.

DRAWING.

1. Draw a square, 5 inches on a side ; in this draw a simple design.

2. Draw an Egyptian or Greek border, writing name underneath.

3. Draw from objects in position, showing actual size.
Ruling and mechanical measurements are not allowed.

ENGLISH.

1. Write a composition of not less than twenty or more than thirty lines on Arbor Day. State (1) what you know of its origin ; (2) why and how it is celebrated ; (3) how it was celebrated in your school ; (4) what wise and useful purpose is attained by its celebration.

(Credit will be given for arrangement, correct use of words, punctuation, and grammatical construction.)

2. (*a*) Give the plural of valley, journey, sheaf, ellipsis, and index. (*b*) Write each of these words in a sentence. (*c*) Write a sentence illustrating antithesis.

3. (*a*) Define the following words : Graphic, scribe, raise, raze, and fare. (*b*) Write a simple sentence containing the word graphic, a compound one with raise, and a complex one with raze. (*c*) Write the two following sentences, using a different gender :
She is an alumna of our College.
She instituted her husband as executor of her will.

4. (*a*) Form three other words from the word origin ; three from court, and three from human. (*b*) Explain the difference between learn and teach, and between famous and notorious. (*c*) Write a complex sentence containing learn and teach.

5. Punctuate and capitalize the following :
There is a highly suggestive sentence in one of matthew arnold's letters which runs thus perfection in the region of the highest poetry demands a tearing of one's self to pieces which men do not readily consent to unless driven by their demon to do so there surely we have the explanation of which

we are in search in eight words though he has left works in verse that will not die thyrsis the scholar gypsy obermann once more etc still at no time of his life did matthew arnold tear himself to pieces he preferred to cultivate tranquillity he wrote some most beautiful poetry but he was not driven by his demon to do so and at length he ceased to write poetry altogether.

GRAMMAR.

1. What is a part of speech? Why do words change from one part of speech to another? How can you distinguish the parts of speech?

2. What is a *passive?* a *redundant?* a *defective* verb? Write three sentences, each containing one of these.

3. Compare *little, well,* and *ill.*

Compare *in, out,* and *up.*

Name three adjectives that cannot be compared, and give reason.

Write a noun clause in apposition with the subject of the sentence, in other words, explanatory of the same.

4. Correct the following sentences and give the reasons:

It is our duty to protect this government and that flag from every assailant, be they whom they may.— *Douglas.*

Burke was offered a very lucrative employment.— *Goodrich.*

Homer, as well as Virgil, were translated and studied on the banks of the Rhine.— *Gibbon.*

While ever and anon there falls huge heaps of hoary moulded walls. — *Dyer.*

5. Write a sentence which has a clause used as a subject.

Write a complex sentence containing both an adjective and an adverb clause. In the following sentence state the kind of sentence; write the clauses; tell the kind of clause each is:

" You'll ask me, why I rather choose to have

A weight of carrion flesh than to receive

Three thousand ducats : I'll not answer that ;
But say it is my humor."
6. Parse *ask, why, rather, receive, that.*

GEOGRAPHY.

1. (*a*) What is the Equator?
  (*b*) Name the Polar Circles.
  (*c*) Give the cause of the change of seasons.
  (*d*) What part of the earth's surface has no sunlight in June?
  (*e*) Why does a telegram sent from New York at noon reach Chicago before noon?
2. (*a*) Bound Manhattan Island, Staten Island, and Long Island.
  (*b*) By what other name is Staten Island known?
  (*c*) Of how many counties is Long Island composed? Name them.
3. (*a*) Name three great railroads running through the State of New York.
  (*b*) Give reasons which justify the term Empire State as applied to New York.
4. (*a*) Bound the State of Maine.
  (*b*) Name its capital, and four important towns.
  (*c*) Where is Harvard University? Yale College? Cornell University?
5. (*a*) Mention five sea-ports in Europe to which steamers leaving New York sail regularly.
  (*b*) Name the four largest islands of the West Indies ; also, the four largest of the East Indies.
  (*c*) Name the bodies of water a ship would pass through in sailing from London to Calcutta.
6. Write the capitals of Holland, Austria, Japan, Canada, Thibet, Persia, Transvaal, Chili, Peru, and Venezuela.
7. Name three great rivers in Africa ; three in South America ; and three in Asia.
8. (*a*) Where are the Aleutian Islands, and to whom do they **belong?**

(*b*) Where is the Island of Formosa, and to whom does it belong?

(*c*) What nations own the following islands: Jamaica, Cuba, Java, Corsica, and Iceland?

UNITED STATES HISTORY.

1. (*a*) Name the three vessels which Columbus commanded when he set forth on his great voyage of discovery.

(*b*) Why was the New World not named after Columbus?

(*c*) By what right did Spain, France, and England claim North America?

2. (*a*) Name the Dutch governors of New York. (*b*) State what you know of the Patroons of the colony of New York.

· **3.** (*a*) What four expeditions moved against the French in 1755? (*b*) Give a brief account of Braddock's expedition against Fort du Quesne. (*c*) What great man was a subordinate officer in this expedition?

4. (*a*) Where and when did Washington take command of the Revolutionary army? (*b*) What important victories did Washington gain at the close of '76 and the beginning of '77? (*c*) Where did Congress assemble while the British occupied Philadelphia? (*d*) In what two battles near Philadelphia were the Americans defeated? (*e*) By what victories in the State of New York was the cause of independence greatly benefited?

5. (*a*) Why did "The articles of Confederation" not furnish a good government for the new Republic? (*b*) When was the present constitution adopted by the States? (*c*) By what vote was it adopted? (*d*) What difficulties led to the establishment of a strong central government?

6. (*a*) What were the Alien and Sedition Laws? (*b*) During whose administration were these laws passed? (*c*) During whose administration and from whom was the Louisiana purchase made? (*d*) What was the Missouri Compromise?

7. (*a*) State the causes which led to the Mexican war. (*b*) What battles were fought by General Scott between Vera Cruz and the City of Mexico? (*c*) Name the territory ceded by Mexico at the close of the war. (*d*) Explain the Fugitive Slave Law. (*e*) What great work written by a woman made abolitionists by the thousand? (*f*) Name the writer.

8. (*a*) State the causes that led to the civil war. (*b*) Name the States which passed ordinances of secession. (*c*) Describe the two flags—the United States and the Confederate. (*d*) What was the first important battle of the civil war? (*e*) Which side was successful? (*f*) Name the chief commanders. (*g*) How often did Lee invade the North? (*h*) In what great battle was he defeated during his first invasion? (*i*) What was the greatest victory gained by the Army of the Potomac? (*j*) Name three of Grant's greatest victories.

9. (*a*) How was slavery abolished in the United States? (*b*) Why was President Johnson impeached? (*c*) Who were the candidates for the presidency in 1876? (*d*) What dispute arose about the election? (*e*) Who was Secretary of State under Garfield?

Spelling.

Horace Mann, *LL.D.*, was born in *Franklin, Norfolk* County, *Massachusetts*, May 4, 1796. His father was a farmer in limited circumstances. The boy earned his school-books by *braiding* straw. At the age of twenty he commenced the study of Latin, and in six months completed his *preparation* to enter the *sophomore* class in Brown University, Rhode Island, where he was graduated with the highest honors in 1819. In 1821 he entered the law school at *Litchfield,* and in 1823 was admitted to the bar. In 1833 he was elected to the State *Senate.* To his enlightened *philanthropy* was due the establishment of the State *Lunatic* Hospital at *Worcester.* In 1837 he was elected Secretary of the Massachusetts Board of Education. By his *diligence, enthusiasm,* and *indomitable* energy he effected a thorough reform in the educational system of the State.

He went bail for a man who stole a bale of cotton.

His gait while passing through the gate was unsteady.

The pale girl carried a pail of water.

Alpaca	Jocund	Venetian
Bilious	Kangaroo	Portuguese
Crustaceous	Lacerate	Spaniard
Dramatize	Larynx	Italian
Ecstasy	Macerate	Cincinnati
Edible	Nautilus	Orinoco
Filament	Ocular	Bartholomew
Ferret	Operatic	Cornelius
Glycerine	Parricide	Dardanelles
Heifer	Quarantine	Tiberius
Inoculate	Sibylline	

College of the City of New York, 1897.

ARITHMETIC.

1. (*a*) What is meant by a quotient? by a minuend?

    (*b*) What is shown by the numerator and what by the denominator of a common fraction?

    (*c*) What is meant by the present worth of a sum of money payable at a future time?

    (*d*) Why are common fractions reduced to a common denominator before they are added?

2. (*a*) What part of $\dfrac{\frac{2}{5} \text{ of } 1\frac{1}{5}}{40\frac{1}{2}\times\frac{2}{3}\frac{0}{3}}$ is $\dfrac{\frac{3}{4} \text{ of } 1\frac{1}{7}}{2\frac{3}{5}\times\frac{2}{13}}$?

    (*b*) Find the value of $1\frac{5}{8}-\frac{3}{17}$ of $4\frac{1}{4}+\frac{1}{8}$.

3. (*a*) What decimal part of a furlong is $\frac{4}{5}$ of a foot?

    (*b*) What is the effect of multiplying the denominator of a common fraction by 3?

    (*c*) Explain the reason of this.

4. (*a*) Write in decimal form: nine ten-millionths; thirty-three ten-thousandths; ten, and twenty ten-thousandths.

    (*b*) Divide .064 by 16; by .00016.

    (*c*) Reduce to a decimal form and add: $\dfrac{3}{1000},\ \dfrac{8}{125},\ \dfrac{121.11}{11}$

5. (a) What is the effect upon the value of a decimal of moving the decimal point one place to the right?

(b) Explain why this is so.

(c) In multiplying one decimal by another, how many decimal places must be pointed off in the product?

(d) Explain the reason for this rule.

6. If it requires $\frac{19}{9}$ bushels of oats to keep 3 horses $\frac{1}{3}$ of a month, how many horses can be fed for $\frac{1}{5}$ of a month, on $\frac{57}{9}$ bushels?

7. A cistern has two pipes (A and B) to fill it, and one pipe (C) to empty it. On one occasion after A and B had both been running for two hours, the cistern was found to be $\frac{1}{3}$ full. Then A and B were turned off, and C opened for two hours, when it appeared that the cistern was $\frac{1}{6}$ full. If then all three had been opened together, how soon would the cistern have been filled?

8. A man who had $2,000 in cash was offered a house and lot for $11,850. He borrowed $5,000 from a friend, giving to his friend his note for $5,000 at six months at 6%. He also had a note at six months discounted at the bank for such a sum as yielded him the remaining $4,850. He then bought the property, and sold it at the end of the six months for $13,500. After he had paid his notes how much had he left?

9. Two mechanics, A and B, undertook a job together, agreeing to share the profits equally. In performing the work, A paid out for wages and material $116, and B paid out for the same $56. A collected the bill in full for $250. How much should he pay to B?

10. A man bought bonds having a par value of $10,000 at 10% discount, held them for one year, receiving during that time 5% interest on them, and sold them at 6% below par. What interest has he made on his money?

ENGLISH.

" Spake full well, in language quaint and olden,
  One who dwelleth by the castled Rhine,
When he called the flowers, so blue and golden,
  Stars that in earth's firmament do shine.

"Stars they are, wherein we read our history,
   As astrologers and seers of eld,
Yet not wrapped about with awful mystery,
   Like the burning stars, which they beheld.—*Longfellow.*

In the above selection, state what is meant by

(*a*) *In language quaint and olden.*
(*b*) *The castled Rhine.*
(*c*) *Earth's firmament.*
(*d*) *Astrologers and seers of eld.*
(*e*) *Wrapped about with awful mystery.*

2. Analyze the first stanza of the selection given above; -classify the sentence, describe each clause, and give the principal parts with their word and phrase adjuncts.

3. Parse *spake, well, quaint, one, flowers.*

4. By means of various prefixes, make from the root of each of the following words two other English derivatives : *aspire, assign, ascribe, deceive, affect.*

5. On a separate sheet of paper, write to a friend in Boston, a letter, of about one hundred words, in which you give an account of Grant Day. Sign your letter Washington Irving.

GEOGRAPHY.

1. What river must one cross in going from (1) Arizona to California, (2) Georgia to South Carolina, (3) Illinois to Iowa, (4) Indiana to Kentucky, (5) Iowa to Nebraska, (6) Louisiana to Texas, (7) Maryland to Virginia, (8) New Hampshire to Vermont, (9) New Jersey to Pennsylvania, (10) Ohio to West Virginia, (11) Oregon to Washington ?

2. Locate these islands and state to what countries they severally belong : (1) Alderney, (2) Corsica, (3) Crete, (4) Helgoland, (5) Jamaica, (6) Joannes, (7) Spitzbergen, (8) Sumatra, (9) Tasmania.

3. Of what larger countries are the following states, kingdoms, provinces, etc., severally parts? (1) Amooria, (2) Bohemia, (3) Chihuahua, (4) Finland, (5) Lombardy, (6) Normandy, (7) Oklahoma, (8) Ontario, (9) Saxony, (10) Syria, (11) Thibet, (12) Victoria, (13) Wales.

4. The daily papers contain advertisements of steamers to sail for (1) Antwerp, (2) Bremen, (3) Genoa, (4) Glasgow, (5) Hamburg, (6) Havre, (7) Hongkong, (8) Liverpool, (9) Rotterdam, (10) Southampton, (11) Yokohama. Tell of each of these ports in what country, and at or near the mouth of what river,, or on what sea, gulf, etc., it lies.

5. When it is noon at Cape Farewell it is midnight near Okhotsk. How far apart are Maranham and the Admiralty Islands (*a*) in degrees and (*b*) in miles? Both lie near the equator, Maranham due south of Cape Farewell, and the Admiralty Islands south of Okhotsk.

6. Where do the Bedouins live? (2) where the Bushmen? (3) where the Choctaws? (4) where the Esquimaux? (5) where the Hottentots? (6) where the Malays?

HISTORY.

1. Briefly describe the voyages and discoveries of the Cabots; of Champlain; of Hudson.

2. Describe the early colonists of New York, Pennsylvania, and Virginia, showing in what respects they differed from each other.

3. How did the French and Indian War differ, in its origin and results, from other colonial wars? Explain the final success of the English.

4. Was the Declaration of Independence a cause of the Revolutionary War? Explain why it was issued.

5. What were the boundaries of the United States, as fixed by treaty, at the close of the Revolution? What additions have since been made, and when and how have they been acquired?

6. Give the leading events of Madison's and Jackson's administrations.

☞ Answer but *one* of the following questions, giving the number of the one you answer :—

7. What are the leading features of the government of the State of New York?

8. What services did General Grant render this country during the Civil War ?

9. State concisely for what the following men have been distinguished in our history : Thomas Jefferson, Daniel Webster, General Greene, Robert E. Lee, Wm. H. Seward.

N. B.—The candidates will also be marked for their SPELLING on this paper. They should examine their work carefully before handing it in.

Normal College.

ARITHMETIC.

1. A cistern has a capacity of $289\frac{1}{11}$ gallons, and has a pipe discharging into it $25\frac{1}{3}$ gallons per hour, and .there is a leak through which it loses $5\frac{1}{4}$ gallons per hour : how long will it take to fill the cistern ?

2. What is the value of $\dfrac{1.2}{7} + \dfrac{37 \times 5000}{200} - \dfrac{7}{8}$?

3. A coal dealer receives $18.68 for 4,624 pounds of coal, what was the price per ton ?

4. The longitude of New York is 74° 3′ west, and of New Orleans 90° west ; what is the difference in time?

5. A student who attended school 75 days during a term was marked 85% for attendance ; how many days was he absent ?

6. The proceeds of a three months note discounted by a bank at 5% were $1,000 ; find the face of the note.

7. How many dollars would a man gain in buying 240 shares (the par value of each share being $100) of railroad stock at $3\frac{3}{8}$ % discount and selling the same at $1\frac{7}{8}$ % premium?

8. If I buy oranges at 15 cents a dozen and sell them at the rate of 3 for 5 cents, what per cent. profit do I make ?

9. If A travéls 24 miles 198 rd. 4 yd. in 6 h. 30 min., how far will he go in 9 h. 45 min. ?

10. How many square feet in the sides of a room 18 ft. long, 14 ft. 6 in. wide, and 9 ft. 6 in. high ?

11. A gold eagle of the United States weighs 258 gr., and the silver in it weighs 25.8 gr.; what per cent. of the coin is silver?

12. A man bought 1,000 shares of stock for $18,000 and sold 800 shares for what they all cost; required the gain per cent.

13. A receives $1,260 dividends at 7%; required the amount of stock he owns and number of shares, each share being $50.

14. What is the longest straight line that can be drawn on the floor of a room 20 ft. 9 in. long and 15 ft. 3 in. wide?

15. Find the cube root of 389,017.

DRAWING.

1. Draw a pentagon 3 inches on a side.

2. Draw a square 5 inches on a side; in this inscribe a circle.

3. Draw any Egyptian or Greek ornament, writing name underneath.

4. Draw a hexagonal prism, placed so that the top is below the level of the eye, and resting on hexagonal face. Height about six inches.

Ruling is not allowed.

ENGLISH.

1. Write a composition of between twenty-five and thirty-five lines on General Grant, stating (1) his full name, (2) his rank in the army, (3) where and when he was born, (4) in what wars he served as an officer, (5) the names of four great battles in which he was victorious, and any other important events in his life you may choose to narrate.

[*Credit will be given for arrangement, correct use of words, punctuation, the use of capital letters, grammatical construction, and accuracy of fact.*]

2. From the word *fame* form four words, and use each in a separate sentence—the first, simple; the second, compound; the third, complex; and the fourth containing two clauses, one adjective and the other adverbial. Name five kinds of words beginning with capital letters.

3. Show the difference between the words *learn* and *teach,*

and illustrate this difference by using both words in the same sentence. When should you use O, and when Oh? Use each in a separate sentence. Put in the plural the two following sentences :

(a) This young man is an Alumnus of the City College.

(b) This young lady is an Alumna of the Normal College.

4. Define the following words : *cite, site, prey, trend, feud.* Give your reasons for approval or disapproval of the following :

(a) Whom do you think I am?

(b) Why don't you lay down and take a nap?

(c) A farmer advertises that boarders will get healthy food on his farm.

5. Capitalize and punctuate :—

a bill after passing both houses is sent to the president who has ten days sundays excepted to consider it if he approves he signs it if he does not approve the bill he usually returns it to the house in which it originated with his reasons for not signing it if he does not return it within the ten days it becomes a law without his signature unless congress has adjourned before the ten days expired

> There rolls the deep where grew the tree
> O earth what changes thou hast seen
> There where the long street roars hath been
> The stillness of the central sea
> The hills like shadows melt they flow
> From form to form and nothing stands
> They fade like mists the solid lands
> Like clouds they shape themselves and go

ENGLISH GRAMMAR.

1. Write three nouns that are alike in both numbers. Give the plural form for tooth-brush, spoonful. State and illustrate the three principal ways of forming gender. Define case. How many cases in English? How do you distinguish each?

2. What rules can you give for the correct use of *shall* and *will?* Write a suitable example of each rule.

3. Parse the italicized words in each of the following :
The staff of his spear was *like* a weaver's beam.
What we *like*, seldom tires us.
He ran *like* a deer.
Forward *like* a blood-red flag the bright flamingoes flew.
It is scarcely worth *while*.

4. Analysis.

> " His hand was known
> In heaven by many a towered structure high,
> Where sceptered angels held their residence,
> And sat as princes, whom supreme King
> Exalted to such power, and gave to rule,
> Each in his hierarchy, the orders bright."

Write out, separately, each subordinate or dependent clause, taking care to supply what is wanting to any elliptical clause. Tell the *kind* of clause according to the divisions known as substantive (noun), adjective, and adverbial clauses.

5. Syntax.

> Full *fathoms* five thy father lies.
> He died the *death* of the righteous.
> My friends said such things *as* surprised me.
> The wall is only a *foot* high.
> This bodes *us* no good.

Parse the italicized words in each of the foregoing.

GEOGRAPHY.

1. (*a*) Name two important islands belonging to the State of New York.
   (*b*) Bound the State of New York.
   (*c*) Name five large cities in New York in the order of their population.
   (*d*) What counties and portions of counties are included in the Greater New York ?
   (*e*) Name two great railroads and one great canal in the State of New York.

2. (*a*) State in degrees the width of each zone.
   (*b*) Name the continents and oceans in order of size.

(c) At what place on the globe must a person be to have the sun in the zenith on the 22d of June ?

(d) What is the situation of places having the same length of day ?

3. (a) Name and locate five cities situated on the great lakes between the United States and British America.

(b) What State of the Union has the largest population ? the largest city ? the greatest commerce ?

(c) Name the States on the west bank of the Mississippi and the capital of each.

4. (a) Name the six great powers of Europe, the capital of each of these countries, and where situated.

(b) Name five islands in the Mediterranean in the order of their size.

(c) What is the most populous empire in the world ?

(d) What is the capital of Persia? of Thibet? of Japan ?

(e) Name the four large cities in Australia.

5. (a) When it is noon at San Francisco, what o'clock is it at St. Petersburg, the former being 124° west longitude, and the latter 32° east longitude?

(b) Name three groups of islands west of Northern Africa.

(c) Name the states along the northern coast of Africa.

(d) Why is there little rain in Northern Africa?

(e) Name five mountain-ranges in Europe and locate them.

HISTORY OF THE UNITED STATES.

1. What was the greatest political event of the American Revolution ? Where and when was the last pitched battle of the Revolution fought ? Where and when the last siege conducted ? What was the result of this siege? Who commanded the French fleet which aided Washington in the last year of the Revolutionary war ?

2. Who was the first Secretary of the Treasury ? What measures did he take to establish the financial credit of the

Jnited States? Who was the first Vice-President? Who vas the first Secretary of War?

3. What was the most celebrated naval battle of the Revolution? of the War of 1812–15? of the Civil War? State the auses of these wars.

4. When and by whom was African slavery introduced into he United States? In what year was the slave trade abolished? What· was the Compromise Bill, and when was it passed? What was the cause of the Mexican War? What territory vas purchased at the close of this war?

5. Explain briefly the Fugitive Slave Law? During whose dministration was this law passed? Explain briefly the Kanas-Nebraska Bill. Who introduced it? By what other name s the Civil War known?

6. Name three decisive battles won by General Grant. What battles were fought by General Sherman between Chatanooga and Atlanta? What was the greatest moral event of he Civil War? Give the date of the beginning and end of his war. Why was President Johnson impeached?

College of the City of New York, 1898.

ARITHMETIC.

1. (a) What is meant by a minuend?
    (b) Give the rule for multiplying one common fraction by another.
    (c) What is meant by the Greatest Common Divisor of several numbers? Give an example.

2. (a) Reduce to its simplest form $\frac{\frac{3}{8}}{\frac{9}{16}}$
    (b) Reduce to a simple fraction
        $\frac{4}{7}$ of $\frac{3}{8}$ of $2\frac{1}{4}$ of 14.
    (c) Add together $\frac{2}{5}$, $\frac{3}{4}$, $\frac{5}{6}$.

3. (a) Reduce $\frac{3}{80}$ to a decimal fraction.
    (b) What part of $\frac{2}{3}$ is $\frac{4}{7}$?
    (c) Find the least common multiple of 24, 12, 180.

4. (a) Write in decimal form: forty-five ten-thousandths; three hundred and one, and sixty-six thousandths; ten thousand, and five hundredths.
    (b) What is the quotient of 6.25 by 2.5?
        What is the quotient of 6.25 by 0.0025?
    (c) Convert .875 into a common fraction and reduce the result to its lowest terms.

5. (a) If the denominator of $\frac{3}{4}$ is multiplied by 5, what effect is produced on the value of the fraction?
    (b) Explain the reason of this.

6. The garrison of a besieged city consisted of 2,000 men, and they had provisions for 8 weeks. After the siege had lasted 3 weeks a re-inforcement of 500 men was received. How long after this would the provisions last?

7. A speculator borrowed $18,000, giving his note at 6%, and invested the money in bonds which he bought at 10%

below par. At the end of 6 months and 18 days he sold the bonds at 5% premium and immediately paid his note with interest. How much money did he have left ?

8. A man spent $\frac{1}{4}$ of his income for house rent, $\frac{1}{4}$ of the remainder for clothing, $800 for all. his other expenses, and had $200 over. What was his income ?

9. A shopkeeper just starting in business, who had $1,000 in cash, borrowed $1,000 from a friend, on a six months' note and had another six months' note for $1,000 discounted at a bank. He invested all the money in goods, and sold them within the six months. · He sold half of these at an advance of 40% on their cost, one third of them at an advance of 30%, but the rest he had to sell at a loss of 5%. When he had paid his notes how much had he left ?

10. What will it cost, at 9 cents a yard, to plaster a room 21 feet long, 18 feet wide and 12 feet high, and which has two doorways each 6 feet wide and 7½ feet high, and two windows each 12 feet high and 6 feet wide ?

ENGLISH GRAMMAR.

1. Analyze the following sentence :
> Home they brought her warrior dead ;
> She nor swoon'd, nor utter'd cry :
> All her maidens, watching, said,
> " She must weep or she will die."

2. In the above sentence parse the following words : *home, brought, dead, watching, will die.*

3. Guilt and misery shrink, by a natural instinct, from *public notice ;* they *court privacy* and solitude : and, even in their choice of a grave, will sometimes *sequester* themselves from the general *population of the churchyard,* as if declining to *claim fellowship* with the great family of man.
Explain the expressions in italics.

4. State the meaning of the prefix of each of the following words : *Circumscribe, infallible, postpone, obstruct, reaffirm.*

State the meaning of the suffix of each of the following : *Successful, magnify, maker, waspish, gosling.*

5. Write a composition of one hundred and fifty words on the Maine disaster.

GEOGRAPHY.

1. Name the three South American republics on the Atlantic Ocean, the two on the Caribbean Sea, the five on the Pacific Ocean, the two inland.

2. Tell in what States and on what rivers these cities severally lie : (1) Bismarck, (2) Hartford, (3) Little Rock, (4) Louisville, (5) Minneapolis, (6) Nashville, (7) Omaha, (8) Poughkeepsie, (9) Topeka, (10) Wheeling.

3. Where (in what ocean or sea, near what land and in what direction from it) are (1) the Aleutian Islands ? (2) the Azores ? (3) the Hebrides ? (4) the New Hebrides ? (5) the Ionian Islands ? (6) the Sunda Islands ?

4. Locate these lakes : (1) Albert Nyanza and Victoria Nyanza, (2) Baikal, (3) Cayuga and Seneca, (4) Como and Maggiore, (5) Great Bear, (6) Great Salt, (7) Ladoga and Onega, (8) Moosehead, (9), Nicaragua, (10) Wener and Wetter.

5. (1) How much of Europe and how much of Asia belong to the Russian empire ? (2) Name the oceans, seas and gulfs, and countries which surround it. (3) How much of the land of the globe belongs to the British empire ? (4) Name its principal colonies and possessions.

6. (1) Why do travelers go to Switzerland ? (2) Why to Egypt ? (3) Why to Naples and its environs ? (4) What scenery, natural formations and phenomena, what buildings and constructions, may travelers in the United States be advised to visit ?

7. (1) On maps the North is usually above, and people usually say "up north" ; what proves that the northern coast of both continents is lower than the land south of it for hundreds of miles ? (2) What is the greatest length of the United

States, from the mouth of the Columbia to the mouth of the St. Croix? and what is the greatest breadth of the country, from the mouth of the Rio Grande to the Canadian border? (3) How great will these distances be on a map drawn on the scale of **1 : 2,000,000**?

HISTORY.

1. Give an account of the settlements of Virginia and Rhode Island.   Include the leading facts, names, dates, etc.

2. Explain the origin of the names (1) "New York," (2) "Georgia," (3) "Baltimore," (4) "United States." State when and how they came to be applied.

3. What Presidents have died in office, and who succeeded them?

4. What European powers claimed parts of North America by right of discovery?   Which one claimed the Ohio region, and when and how did it lose it?

5. Describe the final campaign of the Revolutionary War.

6. Give the Southern and Northern views of the secession question, 1861.

☞Answer but *one* of the following questions, giving the number of the one you answer :

7. State all you know about Andrew Jackson and Abraham Lincoln.

8. When, where and why was the Federal Constitution adopted?   Give a full statement.

9. What powers have had possession of New York City since its first settlement, and state when and why it passed from the control of one to another.

Normal College.

ARITHMETIC.

1. Simplify $\left(\dfrac{3\frac{1}{3}}{7} + \dfrac{2}{10\frac{1}{4}} - \dfrac{15}{18} \times \dfrac{4}{21}\right) \times 1\frac{1}{4}$

2. Find the cost of carpeting a room $25\frac{1}{3}$ feet long and $18\frac{1}{4}$ feet wide with carpet $\frac{3}{4}$ of a yard wide at 75 cents a yard.

3. Divide 45 millionths by 15 and express the answer in words.

4. If 9 persons eat $24 worth of bread in 4 months when flour is worth $6 a barrel, how much bread will a family of 4 persons consume in 5 months when flour is $9 a barrel?

5. Berlin is in 13° 23' 53" E. longitude and San Francisco is 122° 26' 15" W.; When it is noon at the latter, what time is it at the former place?

6. What will 16 cwt. 3 qr 21 lb. cost at $21⅔ per cwt?

7. Find the cost of 136.75 lbs. at $5.50 per ton.

8. A peddler buys oranges at 18 cents a dozen, and sells them at 3 for 5 cents; what per cent. does he make?

9. In how many years will $3,000 amount to $3,438.75 at 2½% simple interest?

10. Paid $54.80 to insure a house worth $30,000, what was the rate?

11. A merchant sells goods at a discount of 15% from the marked price, and still makes a profit of 10%, how many per cent. above cost was the marked price?

12. What is the cost of a draft of $1,000 for 60 days on Chicago, exchange being at 101¼, interest 5% per annum?

13. What is the cost of a draft in Paris on New York for $1,500 when the franc is $.193, premium being 4%?

14. A boy wheels his bicycle 12¼ miles due North and his sister hers 8½ miles due West, how far are they apart? (Carry out to two places of decimals.)

15. What is the face of a note bearing interest at 5% and having 90 days to run that will yield $5,000 if discounted at date at 4%?

DRAWING.

1. Draw a square five inches on a side, and in it any unit of design suitable for a surface covering.

2. Draw any example of Egyptian or Greek ornament, writing the name below.

3. Draw a cube about four inches on a side, the top below the level of the eye, two sides being visible.

4. Draw a square pyramid, the base below the level of the eye and two sides visible ; the base about four inches on a side, the height of the pyramid not less than six inches.

(Ruling and mechanical measurement are not allowed.)

ENGLISH.

1. Write a composition of not less than 100 or more than 150 words on the Spanish-American war, or on Admiral Dewey's victory, or on the battles of Trenton and Princeton.

[*Credit will be given for arrangement, correct use of words, punctuation and grammatical construction, for correct spelling and neat and legible handwriting.*]

2. Define the words *blockade, capitulate, bombard.* Write a compound sentence containing the word blockade, a simple sentence containing the word capitulate, and a complex sentence containing the word bombard. Contract the last sentence into a simple sentence.

3. Write the possessive plural of boy, of hero, of monkey ; the masculine of witch, of spinster, of duck.

. Write the words for which the following abbreviations stand : A.D , Ult., Anon., M.D., and P. O.

4. 1. When is a man said to be " relentless " ? Give its contrary.

2. What is meant by " an indigenous plant " ? Give its contrary.

3. Why is an expression called " ambiguous " ? Give its contrary.

4. When are lines called " convergent " ? What may they be when not convergent ?

5. Fill each of the following blanks with some form of " flee, fly or flow " :

(*a*) The hare — from the hounds.
(*b*) The birds —, as the hunter approached.
(*c*) Before he could fire, they had all — away in the direction of the brook, which — by the meadow.

5. Punctuate and capitalize the following :

Well Ill repent and that suddenly while I am in some liking i shall be out of heart shortly and then I shall have no strength to repent And I have not forgotten what the inside of a church is made of i am a peppercorn a brewers horse the inside of a church company villainous company hath been the spoil of me. .

> God bless the flag and its loyal defenders
> while its broad folds o'er the battlefield wave
> till the dim star wreath rekindles its splendors
> washed from its stains the blood of the brave.

ENGLISH GRAMMAR

1. When are adjectives said to be irregularly compared ? Compare the following words, *ill*, *evil*, *fore*. Write the positive of *further*.

2. For what are verbs inflected ? What is an intransitive verb ? Write one example of a verb ordinarily intransitive with two objects. What is a defective verb? Give an example.

3. Insert the word *only* in four different places in the sentence, *I saw William yesterday*. Tell the part of speech of each *only*, and explain the difference in meaning caused by the change of place in each instance.

4. Classify the following clauses according to the divisions known as noun, adjective, and adverbial :

He is not so courageous as his brother.
I asked him where I could find the horse.
I will buy such things as please me.

He did not enter into the question, how much, truth is preferable to peace.

5. Analyze the following sentence :

> Sleep is a death ; O, make me *try*,
> By sleeping, *what* it is to die,
> And as gently *lay* my head
> On my grave *as* on my *bed*.

State (1) kind of sentence ; (2) write out separately each ubordinate or dependent clause, and no other ; (3) write the ind of clause.

6. Parse the italicized words in the above sentence ; also he italicized words in the following sentences :

(1) He fought the good *fight*.
(2) He walked over a *mile*.
(3) He did nothing but *laugh*. ·

GEOGRAPHY.

1. (*a*) How many great circles can pass east and west around the earth ?
   (*b*) How many can pass north and south ?
   (*c*) Draw a diagram of the zones.
   (*d*) Write on the diagram the names of the boundaries and the width in degrees of each division.
   (*e*) What is the latitude of the North Pole ?
   (*f*) What city in South America has no latitude, and why ?
2. (*a*) Draw a map of the present city of New York.
   (*b*) Write its boundaries.
   (*c*) Write the names of the boroughs on the map.
3. (*a*) What are the largest three cities in the State of New York ?
   (*b*) What State produces the greatest amount of coal ?
   (*c*) Name four other coal-producing States.
   (*d*) Mention the largest four of the West India Islands, and the largest two of the Philippine Islands.
   (*e*) Mention the capitals of. all the States west of the Missisppi.
4. (*a*) What is the form of Government and what is the capital of each of the following countries : *Turkey*, *Canada, France, Japan, British India ?*
   (*b*) Which of these countries has the largest population ?
5. (*a*) What European nations have taken possession of nearly all the African continent ?
   (*b*) How will a fleet sail (taking the shortest route) from Barcelona to Manila, and through what waters would it pass ?
6. (*a*) What part of the Pacific coast of South America has abundant rain ?   ·
   (*b*) What part has none ?
   (*c*) Account for the difference.
   (*d*) What territory of the United States is chiefly desert ?

(*e*) Between what seas is Corea?
(*f*) In what country is the Euphrates River? the Lena? the Irrawaddy? the Amu? the Amoor?

HISTORY (U. S.).

1. 1. For what purpose did the Dutch establish settlements in North America?
2. What name did they give to the country they occupied?
3. To the city at the mouth of the Hudson?
4. What other name was given to this river?
5. By what name was the Delaware known?
6. With what settlement had the Dutch trouble?

2. 1. What was the cause of King William's War?
2. Of Queen Anne's War?
3. Of King George's War?
4. In what respect did the French and Indian War differ from the three wars that preceded it?
5. Mention the treaty that terminated each of the four wars.

3. 1. In what very dangerous condition were Washington and the other leaders of the Revolution prior to the Declaration of Independence?
2. Which was the most important battle of the Revolution, and why?
3. What European nations were represented by great men who assisted the Americans in the Revolutionary War?

4. 1 Under what form of government was the Revolution conducted?
2. What important service was performed by Franklin?
3. Why was it necessary to establish the present Constitution?
4. Into what departments was the Government divided?
5. State the qualifications for a U. S. Senator.
6. For President.

5. 1. What two great victories were gained by the North on the 4th of July, 1863?
2. Who were the opposing commanders in each battle?
3. Name two great admirals, and state what places they captured.
4. State the causes of the following wars:
(*a*) The War of 1812-15;
(*b*) The Mexican War;
(*c*) The Spanish-American War.

College of the City of New York, 1899.

ARITHMETIC.

1. (*a*) Define a prime number. A denominate number. Give examples.
   (*b*) Give the rule for multiplying one decimal fraction by another.
   (*c*) What is the least common dividend of several numbers ?
   (*d*) What is shown by the numerator and what by the denominator of a common fraction ?

2. (*a*) Reduce to its simplest form :

$$\tfrac{4}{7} \text{ of } 1\tfrac{1}{13} \times \tfrac{5}{6} + \tfrac{7}{8}.$$

   (*b*) Add :

$$\tfrac{2}{3} \text{ of } 1\tfrac{1}{2}, \tfrac{5}{6}, \tfrac{11}{12}.$$

3. (*a*) Find the price of 10 lbs. 4 oz. at $10\tfrac{2}{3}$ a ton.
   (*b*) What per cent of 18 is $\tfrac{8}{11}$ of $\tfrac{22}{5}$ of 5 ?
   (*c*) Reduce $\tfrac{1}{1250}$ to a decimal fraction.

4. (*a*) Subtract .003 from 3.0001.
   (*b*) Multiply 3.1 by .031.
   (*c*) Divide 1.6 by .4, by .0004.

5. (*a*) Why is it that multiplying the numerator of a common fraction by a whole number has the same effect upon the value of the fraction as dividing the denominator by that number ?
   (*b*) What effect is produced upon the value of a decimal fraction by moving the decimal point one place to the right ?
   (*c*) Explain the reason of this.

6. If two kinds of coffee are worth 35 and 25 cents a lb. respectively, and chicory is worth 9 cents a lb., what will be the price of 5 pounds of a mixture, 20 per cent of which is coffee of the first kind, 30 per cent coffee of the second kind and 50 per cent chicory ?

7. Ten men can do a piece of work in 8 days. In what time can the work be done by 5 men and 6 boys working together, providing each boy does half as much work as a man in the same time ?

8. A cistern has three pipes. The first can fill it in 4 hours, and the second in 6 hours, while the third can empty it in 3 hours. On one occasion, after the first and second had been running together for two hours, the third pipe was also opened. How long after the third pipe was opened was the cistern full ?

9. A man bought stock having a par value of $20,000 at 15% discount. He held it for six months and received a dividend of 2% during that time. Then he sold it at 12¾% discount. What interest per annum did he make on his money ?

10. A man sold two houses at the same time. For one he received $10,000 cash. For the other he took the purchaser's note at 60 days for $10,500, with interest at 6%, and had it discounted at once at the bank. For which house did he receive the most, and how much ?

English.

I. Analyze both of the following sentences. A diagram is preferred, provided that every relation is clearly indicated and that the sentence and its main clauses are named.

    a.   " Tito was thus sailing under the fairest breeze, and, besides convincing fair judges that his talents squared with his good fortune, he wore that fortune so easily and unpretentiously that no one had yet been offended by it."

b.   "There the common sense of most shall hold a
-a fretful realm in awe,
And the kindly earth shall slumber, lapped in
universal law."

II. From the following passage select all the adjectives,
adverbs and pronouns, write them down separately, and
state the word to which each relates. Write down also all
the finite verbs and all the nouns which are in the nomina-
tive case.

"The Fool, the best of Shakespeare's Fools, made
more conspicuous by coming after the insignificant
Clown in *Othello*, is such an echo—mordantly witty,
marvellously ingenious. He is the protest of sound
common-sense against the foolishness of which Lear has
been guilty, but a protest that is pure humor."

III. Write a letter of two hundred and fifty words from
James Reid, a New York boy, to his cousin, Philip Mon-
tross, who is travelling in Switzerland and who has just
reached Geneva. Write about something that interests you,
such as Dewey day or other recent happenings in the city.

GEOGRAPHY.

1. Name the sea east of Sweden, that west of Alaska, that
south of Cuba, that east of Ireland, that west of Arabia.

2. What river carries the water of the Great Lakes to the
ocean? Which is the largest of the rivers that flow into
the Mediterranean? What rivers flow into the Indian
Ocean (the Persian Gulf, the Arabian Sea, the Bay of Ben-
gal)?

3. Locate these islands—Hondo, Madagascar, Majorca,
Nova Zembla, the Parry Isles.

4. Name the two mountain ranges that separate Asia
from Europe, and the mountains between Tennessee and
North Carolina. Where is the American Sierra Nevada?
and where the European?

5. By what states is Pennsylvania surrounded ?   By what countries Germany ?

6. In what state and on what river is Montgomery ? Sacramento ?   Peoria ?   Dubuque ?   Frankfort ? Augusta ? Detroit ? Bismarck ? Austin ? Richmond ?

7. Locate as definitely as you can, Bahia, Callao, Caracas ; Amsterdam, Brest, Hamburg, Palermo, Southampton ; Calcutta, Shanghai.

8. How many miles is it around the earth on the equator ? How many miles is it from New York to London ?   What is the time at St. Petersburg (longitude 30° E.) when it is noon at London ?

9. What causes winds ?   In what directions do the Trade Winds blow ?   Why ?   Why are they called Trade Winds ?

10. Why are canals built ?   For instance the Suez Canal ? Why is the Erie Canal less important than it was fifty years ago ?   What would be the advantage of the Nicaragua Canal ?

HISTORY.

1. Describe the different kinds of colonial government and give an example of each.

2. When and why did England pass the Stamp Act, and why did the Americans oppose it ?

3. Describe the movements of Washington's army in this vicinity (Greater New York) from August 27, 1776, to November 16, inclusive.

4. Under what circumstances were Louisana and California acquired by the United States ?   Give dates, etc.

5. Name the Presidents who served two terms.   Dates.

6. What services did General Sherman render this country during the Civil War ?

7. Jamestown. Vicksburg, Stony Point : Cartier. Decatur. Meade, Clay.   Why are these names of places and persons prominent in our history ?

Answer but *one* of the following questions, giving the number of the one you answer :—

8. Describe Raleigh's attempt to establish Colonies in America.

9. What are the leading points in the last three amendments to the Constitution of the United States ?

10. What do you understand by the Missouri Compromise ?

Normal College.

ARITHMETIC.

I. Simplify $2\frac{1}{2} \times \dfrac{1}{3\frac{1}{3}+\dfrac{1}{4\frac{1}{2}}}$

II. Two men contract to move a pile of brick for $57.00. The first furnishes 5 carts for 4 days, and the second 3 carts for 6 days. How much should each man receive ?

III. 2 cwt. 8 lbs. is what decimal of 81 lbs. 4 oz. ?

IV. A bankrupt pays $3.76 on every $5 ; what is the dividend on a debt of $17,355 ?

V. Divide 60 into three parts which are to one another as 2, 3, 5.

VI. A house worth $4,000 rents for $275 ; what rate per cent. does this investment pay ?

VII. Five months after date (Dec. 10, 1897) I promise to pay J. C. Thomas $540 with interest at the rate of 6 per cent. per annum. This note was discounted at a bank, April 10, 1898, at 7 per cent. What were the proceeds ?

VIII. What is the face of a bill of exchange in London for which I pay $975.00 in New York, the course of exchange being $4.87½ ?

IX. A commission merchant sold 2140 lbs. of butter at 23 cents a pound. After deducting 5% for his commission and paying $36.50 for freight and charges, and $21.40 for storage, how much should he send the man for whom he made the sale ? •

X. What is the exchange value of a franc when a bill of exchange on New York of $1,500 cost 2,925 francs in Paris ?

XI. I sell two books at $3 each ; on the first I gain 25% and on the second I lose 20%. • How much do I gain or lose ?

XII. What part of an acre is a rectangular piece of land 12 rods long and 132 feet wide ?

XIII. An army lost 18% of its men by sickness and then 14% of the remainder in battle and then contained 84,624 men. What was the original number ?

XIV. A cargo of 400 bushels of wheat worth $1.20 a bushel is insured at $\frac{3}{4}$ of $1\frac{1}{2}$ per cent. on $\frac{2}{3}$ of its value. If the cargo be lost, how much will the owner of the wheat lose ?

XV. One side of a rectangular field is 95 rods long, and the diagonal of the field is 228 rods long. How many acres in the field ?

GRAMMAR.

I. Define *abstract noun, redundant verb, passive verb, voice, defective verb,* and write sentences illustrating each.

II. Write sentences containing an *adverbial clause,* an *adjective clause,* a *noun clause.* Write the possessive plural of *dwarf* and *mouse.*

III. Correct the following sentences and give the reasons : She don't know her lessons as good as formerly.

Wasn't you sorry for her ?

There is a wide difference between a good and bad boy.

The Keepers have strict orders to interfere in every case of the rule against smoking being neglected.

Whom do you think failed yesterday ?

Who did I find in the class-room ?

IV. Analyze the following sentence, stating the kind of sentence, the several clauses and the kind of each :

Th igh we can follow *but* obscurely the Aryan peoples from their common fatherland to their final settlements, we can *yet assert* that the profound differences which are *manifest* between the German races on one side and the Greek and Roman on the other arise for the most part from the difference between the countries in which they have settled.

V. Parse *but, yet, assert, manifest* in the above sentence ; also the italicized words in the following sentences :

Full many a gem of purest ray serene
The dark unfathomed caves of ocean bear.

Cease to do evil : learn *to do* well.

ENGLISH.

I.

In a letter, of from 20 to 30 lines, to a European friend, who has never been in this country, suggest a visit to Greater New York, and mention the principal features of interest to a stranger.

(Credit will be given for arrangement, proper division into paragraphs, punctuation, correct use of words and capitals, and grammatical construction.)

II.

1. State the difference in meaning of : Emigrants and immigrants, diseased and deceased, principal and principle.

2. Write sentences illustrating the proper use of *that*.

    (*a*) as a relative pronoun ;

    (*b*) as an adjective ;

    (*c*) as a conjunction.

3. How would you address the President of the United States ? The Mayor of New York ? A School Commissioner ?

III.

1. Explain the following :

    (*a*) A garrulous person. (*b*) An amphibious animal.
    (*c*) A surgical operation. (*d*) A microscopic object.
    (*e*) An unfathomable depth.

2. What meaning do the prefixes *ante* and *post* impart to the expressions in which they occur ? Give one example for each, in a separate sentence.

3. Define collective noun, and illustrate by a compound sentence.

IV.

Write no less than 14, nor more than 20 lines of a poem you committed to memory.

V.

Capitalize and punctuate properly :

    Just after president mc kinley's inauguration he had his relatives who were in the city at a family dinner at the white house it was a large company and a very good dinner dear old mother mc kinley was there but she was not very talkative she was too happy for words but she kept a sharp eye on the dinner and no detail of it escaped her she was impressed by the quantity of cream served with the fruit and coffee for she looked up at her son in her sweet way and said william you must keep a cow now some of the younger members of the family party found it difficult to suppress a smile but the president with his usual graciousnsss replied yes mother we can afford to have a cow now and have all the cream we can use.

Geography.

I.

(*a*) What is the difference between the polar and equatorial diameters of the earth ?

(*b*) When it was 9 A. M. to-day at Boston, 71° W., what was the time here at New York, 74° W. ?

(*c*) Why do degrees of parallel decrease in length from the equator to the poles ?

(*d*) How many degrees short of the South Pole does light fall on the 21st of June ?

II.

(*a*) Draw a map of Massachusetts.

(*b*) Write its boundaries.

(*c*) Write the names of three cities on the map in their correct positions.

III.

(*a*) What waters does the Erie Canal connect ?

(*b*) Name two reasons for its importance.

(*c*) Name four cities located on it.

(*d*) What States border on the Ohio River ?

(*e*) Name their capitals.

IV.

(*a*) Name the largest State in the Union ; the smallest ; the most populous ; the first settled.

(*b*) Name two States which are chiefly peninsular ; and an important product of each,

(c) Name four States which are chiefly mountainous.

(d) Name four which are destitute of mountains.

V.

(a) Bound Nicaragua.

(b) Why is the Nicaragua Canal important ?

(c) What country in South America has no sea-coast ? in Europe ? In what continent is there no independent State without a sea-coast ?

VI.

(a) Name four European countries which touch the Danube.

(b) What is the form of government of each ?

(c) Name four great rivers which flow from Switzerland into as many countries.

(d) What are the capitals of Holland, Belgium, Hungary, and Greece ?

HISTORY.

I.

1. What idea led to the discovery of America by Columbus ?

2. Give a brief outline of his life (not to exceed seventy words).

3. What sections of this continent were explored by the Spaniards ?

4. What was the cause of Bacon's Rebellion ?

II.

1. Give the principal events in the history of New York from 1664 to 1674.

2. When and where was the first settlement made in Maryland ?

3. What treaties ended King William's War, Queen Anne's War, and King George's War ?

4. Whom did the Indians assist in these wars ?

III.

How did the French and Indian War contribute to the causes of the Revolutionary War ?

When was the battle of Brandywine fought, and who was victorious ?

What important posts on the Hudson were surrendered to the Americans in 1779, and by whom were they taken ?

What European nations were represented by great men who assisted the Americans in the Revolutionary War ?

IV.

What was the cause of Shay's Rebellion ?

In what year and from what place was the seat of government removed to Washington ?

Describe the battle of New Orleans of the War of 1812.

What States were admitted during Jackson's administration ?

V.

When was the battle of Buena Vista, who were the commanders, and which party was victorious ?

When and to whom did the Mexicans surrender Vera Cruz ?

What important question arose at the commencment of Taylor's administration ?

Of which party was Buchanan the candidate.

VI.

By what right did England demand the surrender of the envoys Mason and Slidell ?

Which vessels did the Merrimac destroy at Norfolk ?

Describe briefly the battle of Antietam.

By whom and when was the last invasion of the North during the Civil War ?

VII.

1. What Presidents held office for two consecutive terms ?
2. From whom and for what sum was Alaska purchased ?
3. When and where were international exhibitions held in the United States ?
4. What form of government exists in the State of New York ?

SPELLING.

THE HAGUE, May 19.—One *incident* that *occurred* at the *meeting* was *possibly* of some *significance*. Sir Julian *Pauncefote*, President of the British *delegation* proposed that the subject of *humane regulations* in *extension* of the *Geneva convention* should be *assigned* to two *committees*, one to *consider* naval and the other *military* affairs. The meeting *negatived* the suggestion and decided to refer the whole subject to a single committee. Mr. Andrew D. White of the American delegation *supported* Sir Julian, and the defeat of the *proposition indicates* a line of *cleavage* which will probably *reappear* when other questions arise.

MANILA, May 20, 7:50 A. M.—The Filipino Commissioners on their way to join the other Commissioners were detained because they were not in sympathy with peace negotiations. . . Brigadier-general Funston has relieved General Wheaton.

Alpaca.	Hyacinth.	Proselyte.
Antarctic.	Initiate.	Havana.
Bigoted.	Javelin.	Savannah.
Visited.	Mythology.	Venetian.
Codicil.	Noticeable.	Jamaica.
Dilatory.	Blamable.	Pennsylvania.
Ecstasy.	Parasite.	Sicily.
Halibut.	Porcelain.	Pyrenees.